Writing in English

Book 3

**Anita Pincas,
Gillian and Charles Hadfield**

Macmillan

First published 1982
Reprinted 1983, 1984 (twice)

Published by *Macmillan Publishers Ltd*
London and Basingstoke
Associated companies and representatives in Accra,
Auckland, Delhi, Dublin, Gaborone, Hamburg, Harare,
Hong Kong, Kuala Lumpur, Lagos, Manzini, Melbourne,
Mexico City, Nairobi, New York, Singapore, Tokyo

ISBN 0 333 31763 7

Printed by R. J. Acford, Chichester, Sussex

Typeset in Hong Kong by Graphicraft Typesetters

Acknowledgements
Photographs by Courtesy of
Simon Puttock, Renault and
The British Tourist Authority

Contents

Note: The activity cards used in several of the 'Writing activity' exercises are to be found at the end of the book.

Teacher's notes

Based on *Teaching English Writing* by Anita Pincas (Macmillan, 1982)

1   A brief introduction to the teaching of writing
Writing is an instrument of both communication and self-expression. Most people, however, especially when writing in a foreign or second language, use it primarily to communicate with other members of their own community or the wider world. Our main task is therefore to teach effective functional writing rather than creative self-expression. There are a few initial guiding principles to note:
1   Writing should be as close as possible to genuine functional use of language, as opposed to the traditional set-piece classroom composition for the eyes of the teacher only.
2   Since people's ways of communicating information are very varied, there is no single way of writing correct English. It is therefore important for students to read as widely as possible in order to become familiar with different varieties of written English. They cannot be expected to write in a style which they have never seen or read.
3   Good writing depends on a set of specific writing skills. It does not follow automatically from good grammar and adequate vocabulary.

This book and the other two in this series cover a wide range of functional types of writing. But it is assumed that the practice will be done as part of a normal language course in which students are reading an adequate amount. It is hoped that teachers will supplement the work in each unit by bringing into the classroom as much sample material of written English as they can get hold of, eg English passports, letters, newspaper cuttings, magazine advertisements, official forms and leaflets, posters, etc, in addition to traditional essays and stories.

As far as writing skills are concerned, they can be grouped in three main areas:
I Communicative skills: making the writing functional, ie fulfilling a specific purpose and suiting a specific subject-matter.
For more details, see *Teaching English Writing,* Chapter 2.
II Organisational skills: organising ideas, constructing paragraphs and using linking words.
For more details, see *Teaching English Writing,* Chapter 3.
III Stylistic skills: handling the four major styles (narrative, descriptive, expository, and argumentative), and achieving the right level of formality and the appropriate tone.
For more details, see *Teaching English Writing,* Chapter 4.

The three books in the *Writing in English* series deal with all these skills. Book 1 places emphasis on those areas that relate most easily to elementary grammar and vocabulary. Subject-matter is not too complex for the language available (though it is not childish), and paragraphs are kept short. Narrative has been given some space, but description, exposition and argument are given equal weight. Books 2 and 3 then continue to build up competence in the various writing skills with gradually increasing maturity of English.

2   Grading   The grading of the three books is as follows:
Book I: Vocabulary is limited to the 1800 headwords in *A Learner's First Dictionary* (Macmillan) which is based on criteria of practicality and frequency, and includes all items from the Council of Europe's 'Threshold' syllabus. (For the very few words that go beyond this dictionary, help is usually given by the illustrations, but students should in any case be encouraged to use a native-language/English dictionary.) Structures are limited to those in Stages 1 and 2 of *English Grammatical Structure* by L.G. Alexander *et al*, (Longman, 1975), though not all structures listed there actually appear in the book. As a writing book, *Writing in English* does not aim to practise structures. However the Table of Contents indicates the main structures relevant to each unit, and teachers could therefore usefully link structure drills with the writing practice.
Book II: Vocabulary is limited to the 4700 headwords and derivatives in the Macmillan *New Basic Dictionary*, based on a selection from current lexical surveys and conforming with the Council of Europe recommendations. Structures are limited to those up to Stage 4 in *English Grammatical Structure* (see above).
Book III: Vocabulary is not limited, and students should be competent in using a dictionary by this stage. Structures are limited to those up to Stage 5 in *English Grammatical Structure* (see above).

It is impossible to lay down fixed recommendations about when writing work of this kind should be started. Different educational systems have different requirements and policies, and what might be appropriate in the first year of English in one system might be relevant only for the second or third year in another. It can be said quite unequivocally, however, that as soon as students can handle the level of English in *Writing in English I* they should start writing paragraphs and whole pieces of written English, ie they should move beyond the isolated sentences of their structure drills. Only when they do this are they attempting to use the language in a genuine way.

3   Using this book   All units follow roughly the same plan. Each unit begins with a reading passage which illustrates the type of writing to be taught in the unit. The reading passage is followed by a comprehension task designed to highlight the specific features of the writing which will be taught in the unit. This is followed by a Language Summary which presents these features.

There are usually two tables in the Language Summary. One contains functional language, or useful expressions, while the other contains linking words that will be important in the type of writing under consideration.

The first two exercises in the unit then allow the student to familiarise himself with the new language presented in the Language Summary. Exercises are of well-known types — completion, matching, sentence combining, reordering mixed sentences, etc. But they are not designed to practise vocabulary or structures. They highlight specific writing skills such as the use of linking words, organisation of description, etc.

A number of units also include a reference exercise at this stage. These exercises are designed to provide practice in the use of reference words such as *this*, *these*, *both*, *neither*, *one*, *others*, to link sentences and to avoid repetition — another important writing skill.

The third exercise in each unit introduces the student to the production of text. A paragraph outline provides a plan for the construction of paragraphs, and reordering and guided writing exercises provide practice in recognising how sentences can be organised into text, and in writing from a plan or outline notes.

Exercises 4 and 5 are free writing exercises. The step from controlled or guided writing to free writing is, especially at advanced levels, a large one; while much can be done to prepare the student for the kind of language he may need to use and the kind of organisation he may need to follow, the production of text can never be a merely mechanical activity, but depends on the writer's individual response to his situation and to his audience. At this point in the unit, therefore, an attempt is made to tackle the problem from another direction by providing a context to write in, a stimulus to writing, and an audience to write for. The student will find it easier to write if he has a clear sense of *why* he is writing, and *to whom*. The activities in these exercises, therefore, make much use of pair-work, group work, games, and role play.

The use of group work (which includes writing games) might at first sight appear inappropriate for the teaching of writing. In general, however, *group work* means that there is some kind of cooperation between the members of the class, who are divided into conveniently-sized groups for the purpose. They might be discussing something in pairs before starting to write; they might play a game involving two teams; they might write a letter that another student will have to read and answer; or they might split responsibility among different students so that one student collects information, another organises it and a third actually writes whatever has to be written. Even when group work is not explicitly mentioned in the exercises, teachers should encourage it wherever possible.

(Conversely, most exercises that are set up for group activity in Book 1 can be used for individual work if necessary.)

Moreover, group work can go beyond preparation for writing. The members of a pair, or larger group, can actually *do the writing together*. They can discuss the exact words and sentences to be used, and then either each student writes down what was said, or else they appoint one member of the group to be the writer for all of them. It is always important for the teacher to move fairly systematically around the room, helping each group with vocabulary, making sure everyone is involved, but not staying too long with any group since the main initiative for writing should rest with the students.

Group activity has two practical benefits in the teaching of writing. Firstly, it overcomes the boredom and frequent frustration of traditional methods where each student is sitting silently at his desk, racking his brains for something to write. Secondly, it provides a situation in which students have to communicate with each other, both in speech and writing. Students are then writing for a real reader, not just for the critical eyes of the teacher. Having a real reader will help them to see their writing from the point of view of the person who receives it — they will be forced to consider whether it is clear enough and will soon discover whether it was successful or not for the purpose of the activity.

As for games, needless to say they should be lively and enjoyable. This means that students should not be too much inhibited by the fear of making mistakes. Teachers will find that adults quickly adapt to games as long as their purpose in the writing lesson is clear and they do not overshadow what the students feel to be their main objectives. For more discussion of games see *Teaching Techniques in Communicative English* (J. Revell, 1982) and *How to Use Games in Language Teaching* (S. Rixon, 1982). Both are in the Macmillan Essential Language Teaching Series, Ed. R.H. Flavell.

There is further discussion of teaching methods for familiarisation, controlled/guided and free writing, in *Teaching English Writing*, Chapters 1, 5, 6, 7 and 8. See particularly Chapter 5 which offers a blueprint for the preparation of further exercises.

4 Notes on individual units The teacher can work through the units in two ways. The exercises may be used in the order in which they appear in the units, following the traditional progression from model to presentation to controlled practice to guided practice to free writing.

Alternatively, a cyclical approach may be adopted, and the 'Writing activity' in Exercise 5 placed first. The students should carry out the role play, game or discussion suggested in the activity and then prepare a first draft of the writing task. They can then work through the exercises in the unit, returning to and rewriting their draft at the end of the unit. This approach has much to recommend it. By giving the students a task to carry out before providing them with any new linguistic input, the teacher is offering a communication challenge: the students will have to stretch the language they already possess to the limit. The teacher will then be in a position to diagnose the areas in which the students need most help, and to focus accordingly on the exercises which seem most suitable. It should be possible to individualise work at this stage: some students may not need to do all the exercises, some may need more help or practice in certain areas. Similarly, the student will see the relevance of the exercises he is asked to do, and the correction and improvement of the first draft is a valuable exercise in self-monitoring.

In the notes on each unit, suggestions for preparatory exercises and further work are given. The notes on preparatory exercises include suggestions for revision of the main structures occurring in the units, and for vocabulary enrichment. The exercise notes on further work include suggestions for longer essays, class projects, or the relation and transfer of what has been taught in the unit to other topic areas.

In all the exercises, but perhaps most in the *further work*, teachers will have to make decisions about how much error to allow uncorrected. Current opinion is that only errors related to the teaching aim of the exercise should be remarked upon. See *Language learners and their error* (J.A. Norrish, 1982) in the Macmillan Essential Language Teaching series.

Unit 1

This unit practises character description of the kind found in character references and handwriting analyses, ie an analysis of personality. More 'literary' character description will be found in Unit 6. The distinction between 'positive' and 'negative' characteristics is an important one, as this affects the expressions used to describe character. 'Tends to', for example, is only used of negative characteristics.

Some revision of uses of the present perfect, and some vocabulary work on nouns and adjectives for character description could usefully precede the unit. The vocabulary exercise following the reading passage could be extended by discussing synonyms and opposites for the words in the table.

Exercises 1 and 2 provide practice in using the linking words and expressions from the Language Summary. They should be done individually, but students may compare and discuss their answers in pairs when they have finished. Exercise 3 provides an outline for writing character references. Exercise 3(i) may be done individually.

Exercise 4 could be set for homework. If done in class, students could discuss the questions orally in pairs before writing.

Exercise 5(ii) will be more amusing if the students choose unusual jobs.

Further work Activity 5(ii) could be expanded into an extended role play where students play the parts of employee, his present employers and new employers.

Divide the class into two groups and tell them they represent two large firms. Each group should decide what kind of company they are and what each person's job is within it. Then tell the firms that they both have a vacancy and are advertising for someone to fill it. They decide on the job, and the qualities they are looking for in the candidates for it. They then write an advertisement for the job. The two firms exchange advertisements, and everyone should apply for the job with the other firm. They all write letters of application for the job, and obtain a reference from someone else in their own firm. The letters and references should then be 'posted' to the other firm, who should compare the candidates and discuss their suitability for the post. Interviewing panels can then be set up and interviews held.

Unit 2

The unit concentrates on the use of linking words to express sequence in narrative, and the ways in which the passive is used in narrative.

Preliminary exercises could include a general revision of past simple, past continuous and past perfect tenses, and the use of the passive.

Exercise 1 practises the use of linking words to indicate sequence, and Exercise 2 practises the use of the passive in narrative. These exercises may be done individually or in pairs or groups.

Exercise 3 practises writing topic sentences in narrative. Introducing a report of a long sequence of events with a brief summary makes the report clearer and easier to read. The 'Guided writing' exercise provides practice in organising and summarising information from different sources. Exercises 4 and 5 provide a context and stimulus for writing.

Further work A class newspaper.
(i) The reports written up for Exercise 5 can be collated to form the front page of a newspaper.

The activity can be made more exciting if the students are given a deadline to write up their notes as reports and to prepare the front page.
(ii) The students prepare their own newspaper, with anecdotes, accounts of things they have done, etc. This newspaper could be built up slowly over a period of time. The units on 'Telling a Story', 'Advice', 'Opinion Polls', 'Speeches', 'Changes', and 'Letters to the Editor', should provide more material.

Unit 3

It would be a good idea to precede this unit with some work on uses of the present perfect.

The unit deals with letters of protest and complaint, and the Language Summary introduces expressions for protest and complaint. Some discussion on formality will be necessary here. For instance, 'I feel I must protest/complain', is a fairly strong beginning to a letter, and is usually only used about very annoying behaviour.

As a recognition exercise, students could underline these expressions where they appear in the reading passage. Exercise 1 provides practice in using linking words to join sentences. Exercise 2 provides practice in using expressions of protest and complaint. Emphasise that the students should choose a mild or strong expression according to the context. For the last sentence of the letter they should invent their own suggestions for action, and choose an appropriate phrase from the Language Summary to introduce them.

The exercises may be done individually or in pairs. In Exercises 4 and 5 a short role play provides a context for writing. When the letters of complaint have been written, students could exchange letters and write replies.

Further work Everyone has something to complain about! The students could write letters about something that is annoying them: faulty goods, a neighbour's irritating habits . . . .

Unit 4

This unit, like 'Sci Fi' and 'Beginnings and Endings', has no specific linguistic teaching point, but practises story-telling skills. It deals with pace, variety, and suspense. The students are not, of course, expected to write like Saki but through thinking about what makes a good story, it is hoped that they will find some ways to liven up their own writing. Preparatory work should consist of general revision of past tenses.

The exercises are best done in small groups. In each exercise the teacher should introduce the topic and allow the groups to discuss the questions on their own for a time, before bringing them together in a class discussion.

The stories could also be written in groups if the students work well this way.

Further work Pictures are a useful way of stimulating the imagination and providing a starting point for stories. The students could be given a series of pictures and asked to find links between them and to arrange them in sequence to form a story. Alternatively, an interesting or unusual picture could be used as a starting or finishing point for a story, and the students asked to imagine what happened next or how the characters came to be in that situation.

Unit 5

The unit practises describing cause and effect sequences which are often important in narrative.

Helpful preliminary work would include revision of the use of the past continuous for interrupted actions, and the use of present participles.

The reading passage in this unit is not a model text but a stimulus for role play and writing, although it does contain examples of language presented in the Language Summary.

Students could be asked to look for these examples, and to underline them where they occur in the text. Exercise 1 involves practice in describing situations, and Exercise 2 in combining sentences to show cause and effect relationships. The exercises may be done individually and discussed in pairs afterwards. Exercise 3 provides an outline for a police report, and diagrams for guided writing. Students should work in pairs, discussing the pictures orally before writing. In Exercise 4 the students return to the dialogue between Roadhog and Gardener and build on it, each inventing reasons to blame the other for the accident.

Exercise 5 is a role play where all the participants have different accounts of an accident. Allow the students five minutes to study their cards before beginning the role play. Clear a space in the classroom for the students to move about during the activity.

Further work The work done on cause and effect in this unit could be extended into other topic areas. Students could be asked to write an account of a disastrous day, for example, or provide a lengthy excuse for not arriving at a meeting or party. On another level, historical narrative often involves describing a cause and effect chain. Students could be asked to write an account of an important chain of events in the history of their country.

Unit 6

The unit practises describing people in a rather more 'literary' way than Unit 1. The focus is on describing appearance and behaviour, on ways of organising description, and on avoiding monotony by varying sentence structure.

Useful preparation for this unit would include revision of relative clauses and work on vocabulary for describing people. Magazine pictures of people can be brought in and used as teaching aids. The following game is a good introduction: the students stand in a circle, facing each other in pairs. They have two minutes to study each other's appearance. They then turn their backs on their partner, so that they are facing a new partner to whom they describe the first partner.

Exercise 1 is a vocabulary exercise. Students ought to be familiar with adjective order by this stage but this could be discussed before they do the exercise. Students should complete the exercises individually and compare their results in pairs or small groups afterwards. A class discussion on the different possibilities for filling in the blanks might be profitable.

Exercise 2 aims to provide practice in making descriptions less monotonous by varying sentence structure. Students can work individually and compare results.

The third exercise involves organising description. The point here is that a description of a person should make the character come alive for the reader by making him feel he is getting to know the character. Exercise 4 may be done as an oral discussion in pairs or small groups while the teacher circulates, offering help and comment.

Exercise 5(i) is to be done in pairs. When the students have finished writing, the teacher can collect the descriptions, give each a number and pin them to the wall. Students then walk round the class, matching names and numbers.

For Exercise 5(ii), the teacher can prepare slips of paper with the names of famous people. These can then be dealt out at random.

Further work Character descriptions from stories or novels could be brought in and discussed. If further writing practice is needed, extracts of character description from novels could be used as a stimulus. The students should imagine they know the character concerned, and continue the description.

Unit 7

This unit deals with letters asking for and giving advice, and highlights two features of such letters: useful expressions for advice and recommendation, and linking words for reason-giving. Preliminary work could include revision of *should, would, ought to*.

After presenting the first Language Summary, a short discussion on appropriacy would be useful. The expressions given in the table are all suitable for fairly formal letters. A letter to a close friend might contain phrases like 'What do you think I should do?', 'Can you help me?', and a recommendation from a close friend might contain expressions such as 'If I were you I'd ....', 'I think you should ....'.
After presentation of the Language Summary, students should underline the expressions where they appear in the reading passage.

Exercise 1 may be done individually or in pairs. Students should invent their own reasons for the advice they give. In Exercise 2, students should refer to the Language Summary and choose expressions to begin and end the letters. Exercise 3 provides outline guides for writing letters of advice and recommendation and organising a passage of reason-giving.

The sentences in the reordering exercise are split in half and need to be joined. Exercise 4 has already been prepared orally and should now be done individually. Exercise 5 is a role play providing a context for letter-writing.

The reference exercise in this unit provides practice in the use of abstract nouns such as *situation, matter, circumstances*, to refer back or forwards.

Further work Real problem-page letters from a newspaper or magazine could be brought in and discussed.

Unit 8

The unit deals with the organisation of place description and highlights such features as focus, and the inclusion of both static and moving elements. Preliminary work

should involve some teaching or revision of vocabulary for place description. Magazine pictures or postcards may be brought in as teaching aids.

Exercises 1 and 2 provide practice in using linking words for place relations, and in livening up description by including verbs of movement. The exercises may be done in pairs, with an oral discussion preceding the writing. Exercise 3 deals with organisation of description. The question of *focus* is all important here. If a description contains random, scattered elements, it will be hard to visualise. Exercise 4 may be done individually or in small groups. Oral discussion should precede the writing.

Exercise 5 practises organising a description so that it is easy to visualise. The presence of an audience will make this easier for the student.

Further work Magazine pictures or postcards will provide a stimulus for further writing. Descriptions from novels and tourist brochures could be brought in and the differences in styles and effect discussed.

Unit 9

This unit practises ways of expressing similarities and differences, and of organising comparisons. Preparatory work should involve revision of comparatives. Articles from consumer magazines such as *Which?* could be brought in and studied as preliminary reading.

Students should underline expressions presented in the Language Summary where they appear in the reading passage.

Exercise 1 practises using linking words for comparison in a text. If extra practice is necessary, a similar passage can be written about the two cars in Exercise 2.

In Exercise 2 the students are asked to write ten sentences of comparison about the two cars. The sentences do not have to form a text. The exercise could be prepared orally in class.

Exercise 3 provides plans for two different ways of organising comparisons and practice in using both of them. Exercise 4 may be done individually or in small groups.

The articles produced in Exercise 5 could be collated to form a class consumer magazine. In the reference exercise, possible alternative forms are *both/neither/all/ none of them, all four, none of the six*.

Further work Work on comparisons could be extended into many different topic areas. Students could compare their different lifestyles, daily routines, tastes, upbringing, etc. In a multilingual class, aspects of life in different countries could be discussed. In each case, a small group discussion on a particular topic could lead to a piece of writing.

Unit 10

A general revision of past tenses and vocabulary for describing places and objects could usefully precede this unit. The unit, like the other narrative units, 'Telling a Story', and 'Beginnings and Endings', has no specific linguistic teaching point but is concerned with ways of making narrative livelier and more interesting, in this case by combining narrative and description. The comprehension task of reordering the reading passage will involve recognition of time-links such as *after, then, while, now,* and reference words such as *they, the* and *this* should be pointed out to the students.

Exercise 1 may be done initially in pairs and then as a class discussion. Exercise 2 may be done individually or as a group effort. Exercise 3 provides practice in telling a story orally. The storyteller can judge the reactions of his audience and alter pace accordingly. Create some atmosphere for the ghost stories! Exercise 4 may be done individually or in groups. Exercise 5 is a cooperative activity.

Further work Science Fiction stories may be brought in and discussed.

Unit 11

Like 'Sci Fi' and 'Telling a Story', this unit practises ways of enlivening narrative.

The questions on the reading passage should be discussed in pairs, leading to a class discussion. Exercises 1 and 2 may be done in pairs or small groups. Exercise 3 should be done individually and then discussed in pairs. Exercise 4 can be done individually or in groups, while Exercise 5 is for individual work leading to pairwork and discussion.

Further work The beginnings of various novels could be brought in and shown to the students. The students could discuss them and try to guess how the story continues. Alternatively, a short story could be read to the students, minus the final paragraph. The students can then write their own endings for the story. These can be compared with the actual ending, and discussed in small groups.

Unit 12

The unit deals with hypothesis and focuses on expressing degrees of certainty, and relating hypothesis and evidence. Useful preparation could involve revision of conditionals and modals.

The comprehension task following the reading passage is best done in pairs or small groups. It should lead to further discussion about the murder, and hypothesis about the murderer.

Exercises 1 and 2 provide practice in the use of modal verbs to express certainty, and in the use of linking words for hypothesis and evidence. The exercises may be done in pairs. Exercise 3 provides a plan for the logical arrangement of hypothesis and evidence in a report, and outline notes for a model report. Exercises 4 and 5 provide further practice in organising hypothesis and evidence. These exercises may be prepared orally in pairs or small groups first.

Further work Work on hypothesis and evidence lends itself to other topic areas. Reference could be made to the science-fiction unit, and students could write hypothetical reports about the inhabitants of the planet based on the evidence they have collected. Archaeology is another possible area. Students could prepare a list of objects that an archaeologist might find two thousand years from now. They could then discuss what hypotheses he might formulate about our civilisation, and write up a report of their conclusions.

Unit 13

This unit deals with giving, noting and reporting speech. Preliminary work should include a revision of tenses in reported speech. The Language Summary gives some ground rules for note-making, and also lists linking words for argument. These words mark the different sections of an argument and will signal a change of subject and a new heading. Students could underline these expressions where they appear in the reading passage.

Exercise 1 provides practice in making notes under headings. The exercise may be done in pairs, with one student reading the speech aloud while the other makes notes as he talks. Students could then try giving the speech from the notes they have made. Exercise 2 provides practice in selecting the correct verb of saying in a passage of reported speech.

The paragraph outline shows how to organise an argument. Students could discuss how the sentences in the reading passage fit into this plan. The exercises that follow provide practice in organising arguments under headings.

Exercises 4 and 5 provide a context for writing, giving and reporting speeches. During the preparation time, the teacher should circulate, offering help where necessary. The speeches themselves could be recorded and played back to the students, with feedback and comment.

Synonyms for the words in the reference exercise can be found in the reading passage.

Further work A debate provides a good opportunity for writing and giving speeches. It could be organised either as a class activity or in small groups.

Unit 14

The unit deals with process description highlighting such features as the use of the passive, and linking words for purpose. It is important to emphasise to students that the passive is used to remove *personal subjects* to give a more formal and impersonal tone. Thus, not all verbs in a process description will be in the passive. Revision of passives would be a useful preparatory exercise for this unit.

The first two exercises provide practice in the use of the passive and purpose clauses, and the third concentrates on the use of sequencing links to order a process description. The fourth exercise is a free writing exercise, while the fifth makes use of oral explanation as a preparation for writing. The reference exercise practises the use of *this* and *these* to refer back. The sentences in this exercise could all also be rewritten using purpose clauses.

Further work The students may be set a project in which they find out and write about any industrial or agricultural processes that are important in their country.

Unit 15

The unit deals with describing graphs and reporting changes, and teaches expressions of increase and decrease and linking words to express duration of time. Preliminary work could involve revision of the contrast between past simple and present perfect.

After presentation of the Language Summary, students should underline the phrases from the summary where they appear in the reading passage.

Exercise 1 provides practice in recognition and comprehension of expressions of increase and decrease and time links, while Exercise 2 provides practice in their use. The exercises may be done in pairs or small groups. Exercise 3 outlines two different methods of organising reports. Students could work in pairs on this exercise, each choosing a different outline and comparing the results afterwards. Exercise 4 may be done individually, whereas Exercise 5 involves a class survey to provide the data for a report. The reference exercise in this unit teaches the use of *former, latter, both*, and *neither*, to refer back.

Further work Any graphs, statistics or tabulations brought in by the teacher could provide the basis for further work. In addition, the language and organisation taught in the unit will prove useful for more general, less precise essays, such as a description of the changes in a town or in people's lifestyles over a period of years.

Unit 16

The unit deals with argument, and introduces phrases of approval and disapproval and linking words for concession, addition and refutation. Letters from real newspapers could be brought in and discussed as a preliminary activity.

After presentation of the Language Summary students should underline the expressions where they appear in the reading passage.

Exercise 1 practises perceiving relationships between ideas and using appropriate linking words. Exercise 2 practises introducing and concluding arguments, and Exercise 3 provides an outline for constructing arguments. The letters in the reading passage could be re-read at this point to see how they fit the plan. Exercise 4 is a free writing exercise for individual work, while Exercise 5 consists of a role play to provide a context

for writing. Students should prepare their roles in pairs, thinking of other arguments to defend their positions besides those on the cards. The reference exercise deals with the use of *this/these* and synonyms, and *such/such a* to refer back. Emphasise that 'such' is formal and dignified in tone.

Further work Students could work on a Letter Page for a newspaper, with various letters expressing opinions about aspects of life in their town. Work could be done on longer essays, expressing more than one point of view, or summarising arguments for and against. The opposing viewpoints in Exercises 2, 3, 4 and 5 could be used as the basis for essays of this kind.

Unit 17

This unit deals with the organisation of generalisations and facts in a survey report. Preliminary work could involve the study of opinion polls or statistical reports taken from newspapers. The Language Summary introduces useful expressions for proportion, and ways of linking fact and generalisation. These expressions should be underlined where they appear in the reading passage. Exercises 1 and 2 practise the use of these expressions at sentence level. The exercises may be done individually or in pairs. Exercise 3 deals with the organisation of generalisation and fact in a text. The exercises should be discussed in pairs and then written up. Exercise 4 should be discussed in small groups before any writing is done. In Exercise 5, the students should prepare their questionnaires individually or in pairs, and then walk around the class, interviewing each other. The subjects may be prepared by the teacher beforehand, written on slips of paper and dealt out to the students at random to ensure that everyone gets a different subject. The reference exercise in this unit deals with the use of *that* and *those* to refer back in comparisons.

Further work Could be based on surveys, facts and figures and statistical reports taken from newspapers. Students could do a larger survey project of their own, interviewing people on the street about certain subjects, and writing up the results.

Unit 18

The unit practises the writing of formal proposals and suggestions, and ways of organising a list of features in a description. Preliminary work should involve revision of *should* and *would*.

Exercise 1 practises the use of linking words for purpose. *For + -ing* is always instrumental, ie describing the use of a machine or instrument, whereas *to + infinitive* may be used as a general purpose link.

Exercise 2 practises the use of *would* and *should* in proposals. These exercises may be done individually and compared in pairs. The third exercise presents different ways of organising an object description: features can be grouped under headings or listed in order of importance. Exercise 3(ii) can be prepared orally in pairs before writing: each student should take one picture and describe it to his partner before writing. Exercise 4 may be done individually or in groups, while Exercise 5 is a cooperative activity.

Further work Work on proposals could be extended from fantasy into real life. Students could write proposals for various improvements to their towns, local amenities, schools or colleges.

Unit 1 Character references

Organising a description

Similarities and differences

Reading   Look at this chart on handwriting, and do the exercise which follows.

t

A crossed 't' shows a conscientious and well-balanced person.

mum

Rounded tops indicate a pleasant and cooperative person.

i

Dots to the left show caution.

l

An uncrossed 't' shows laziness.

t

A 't' bar on the right indicates enthusiasm and a quick temper.

i

Dots to the right show generosity.

i

An undotted 'i' shows absent-mindedness.

i

Firm dots show efficiency.

y g

Square loops indicate an aggressive and obstinate person.

l h

Round loops show sensitivity and imagination.

a

Letters open at the bottom indicate a dishonest person.

M l

Angular tops show immaturity.

h l

Letters without loops show independence.

t

A wavy bar tells us the writer is good natured and has a sense of humour.

a

Letters open at the top mean frankness.

Do this activity in pairs. Look at the three examples of handwriting below and discuss them with your partner. What is each writer like? Now read the three character references. Can you match each character reference with one of the samples of handwriting below? Fill the name of the person in on the character reference.

Caroline Watts

Gillian Ketterton

Pat Biggs

(i) . . . . has worked with us for five years and we are sorry to see her go. She has always worked conscientiously and efficiently. She shows imagination; she makes well-balanced decisions, and copes well with new situations. She has a very pleasant personality. We therefore recommend her to you, and wish her well in her future career.

(ii) . . . . has worked with us for about eight months, and has not made a good impression. She tends to be lazy, and is consistently uncooperative. Her manner is obstinate and can be on occasions rather rude. I regret to say that we cannot in all honesty recommend her for a position with your company.

(iii) . . . . has been with the company for eighteen months now. She is somewhat absent-minded and a little immature, but very good natured and pleasant. She is an imaginative and stimulating member of the team, and her sense of humour has been a great asset.

In the handwriting chart the writer sometimes uses nouns and sometimes uses adjectives to describe character.

(i) In the table below, only one form of the word is given. Complete the table with the corresponding nouns or adjectives, using the comments you have just read to help you.

(ii) Which qualities are *positive* and which are *negative*?

Nouns	Adjectives
balance	_____
good nature	_____
_____	absent-minded
quick temper	_____
_____	enthusiastic
_____	generous
dishonesty	_____
_____	cautious
_____	sensitive
_____	immature
_____	imaginative
aggression	_____
_____	frank
_____	independent
conscientiousness	_____
cooperation	_____
_____	efficient
obstinacy	_____

LANGUAGE SUMMARY

1 Describing people: character

The following tables summarise some ways of describing character. These expressions may be used to describe either *positive* or *negative* qualities.

He She	is	cheerful. aggressive. pleasant.	
She He	has a/an	cheerful aggressive pleasant	nature. temperament. disposition. character. personality.
Her distinctive characteristics are obstinacy and selfishness.			

3

These expressions, which are more hesitant, are only used for *negative* qualities.

	has shows	a	strong slight noticeable	tendency to	
He She	tends to				be untidy.
	can	often sometimes on occasions occasionally			

2 Linking words for description: similarities and differences
When a person has two *similar* qualities (both positive or both negative), you can relate sentences like this:

She has a very generous disposition	. She is also very good humoured. and is also very good humoured. , and is very good humoured as well. , as well as being very good humoured.

When a person has two *contradictory* qualities (one positive and one negative), you can relate sentences like this:

He is	usually generally	good natured	, but . In spite of this, . Nevertheless, . However,	he is sometimes obstinate. he can be obstinate. he has a tendency to be obstinate.
Although he is usually good natured, he		tends to can	be	obstinate at times.

Exercise 1
Completion
Look at the handwriting sample below and then choose the right adjective to complete description (i) opposite. Use the handwriting chart to help you. Do the same for (ii) and then fill in the blanks in description (iii).

(i)

Anthony May

4

This man is $\left|\begin{array}{l}\text{good natured}\\\text{quick tempered}\end{array}\right|$. He has a tendency to be

$\left|\begin{array}{l}\text{absent-minded}\\\text{obstinate}\end{array}\right|$ and has a/an $\left|\begin{array}{l}\text{aggressive}\\\text{cautious}\end{array}\right|$ personality. There is

also an element of $\left|\begin{array}{l}\text{immaturity}\\\text{frankness}\end{array}\right|$ in his character.

(ii)

Her distinctive characteristics are $\left|\begin{array}{l}\text{sensitivity}\\\text{efficiency}\end{array}\right|$ and

$\left|\begin{array}{l}\text{imagination}\\\text{obstinacy}\end{array}\right|$. Although she tends to be $\left|\begin{array}{l}\text{absent-minded}\\\text{immature}\end{array}\right|$,

she has a $\left|\begin{array}{l}\text{pleasant and cooperative}\\\text{generous and independent}\end{array}\right|$ nature. She is

$\left|\begin{array}{l}\text{good humoured}\\\text{well balanced}\end{array}\right|$ and has an $\left|\begin{array}{l}\text{open}\\\text{independent}\end{array}\right|$ attitude to life.

(iii)

. . . . is rather . . . . He
tends to be . . . . and is . . . .

Exercise 2
Combining

(i) Join the following sentences using linking words from the language summary.

---

1 He is a very enthusiastic person. He is humorous.
2 He has a rather sensitive nature. He is very imaginative.
3 He has a pleasant and cooperative personality. He tends to be a little absent-minded.
4 She has a generous nature. There is an element of immaturity in her character.
5 He is independent. He can be aggressive.
6 She is usually good humoured. She can on occasions be rather obstinate.
7 He is enthusiastic and good natured. He is rather immature.
8 She is very balanced. She is very kind hearted.
9 He is very efficient. He is conscientious.
10 She has a frank and open character. She tends to be rather too outspoken.

5

(ii) Rewrite these descriptions using linking words to join the sentences.

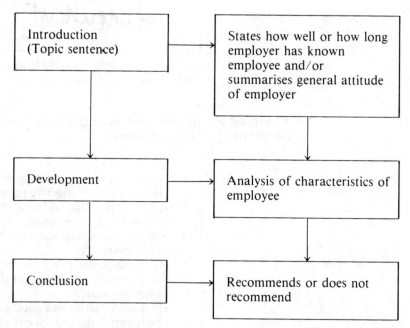

Anna Higgins

This person is rather immature. She tends to be obstinate. She can on occasions be rather aggressive. She is frank and open. She has, on the whole, a generous nature.

Pat Simmonds

Pat is a conscientious and well-balanced person. Her distinctive qualities are efficiency and neatness. She has a pleasant and cooperative personality. She shows a good deal of independence.

PARAGRAPH OUTLINE   This outline shows how the character references in the reading passage are constructed:

Introduction
(Topic sentence) → States how well or how long employer has known employee and/or summarises general attitude of employer

Development → Analysis of characteristics of employee

Conclusion → Recommends or does not recommend

Exercise 3
Rewriting   (i) The following character references are in muddled order. Use the paragraph outline above to help you rewrite them in a more logical order.

We have found him, on the whole, to be rather lazy, and lacking in motivation.

I regret to say that we cannot recommend him for a position with your company.

Mr. Ross has been with the firm for about eight months and has not made a very good impression.

He is consistently late for work, is unwilling to make any effort, and shows little initiative.

He also tends to be rather uncooperative and can be stubborn on occasions.

He has been a hardworking member of the team, showing energy, enthusiasm, and inventiveness.

Mr. Carter has worked with us for ten years now, and we very much regret his departure.

We feel, therefore, that he is admirably suited for the position of manager with your company and have no hesitation in recommending him to you.

He also has a very practical mind, and the ability to make sound decisions.

The improvements he has made in the running of the company have been imaginative and far-reaching.

Guided writing (ii) Use these outlines to write character references for the following people:

Miss Grant

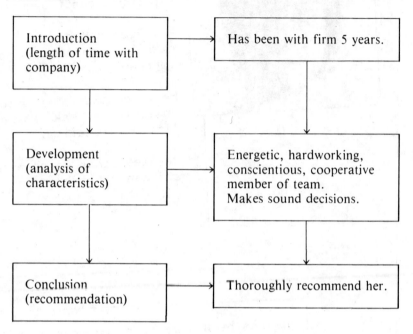

Mr Biggs

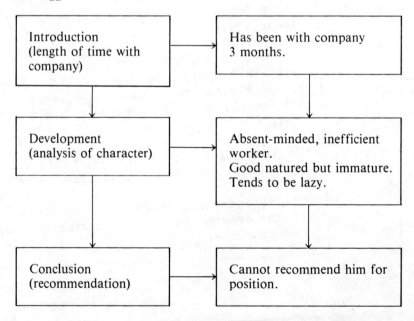

Exercise 4
Free writing

(i) Write a character analysis for each of these samples of handwriting.

(ii) What kind of job do you think each of the writers would be suited to? Write them a character reference for the job.

Exercise 5
Writing activity

(i) Write your name and address on a piece of paper and then pass it to another student.
Write analyses of each other's handwriting.

(ii) Write the name of a job (such as nurse, teacher, thief, President of the USA, bus driver, etc) on a piece of paper.
The teacher will collect them up and redistribute them.
When you have a new piece of paper with a job written on it, ask the person sitting next to you to write you a reference for that job.

Consider:
1   the qualities necessary for the job
2   the characteristics of the person applying
3   his/her suitability for the job.

Unit 2 Front page!

Reporting events

Organising a narrative chronologically

Reading

The passage below is a newspaper report of a raid on a Securicor van (a security van carrying money). Read the passage and do the exercise which follows:

Gunmen grab £1m in security van raid

SIX men armed with rifles and shotguns escaped with £1,014,005 in notes after ambushing a Securicor van on a country road near Chatham, Kent, yesterday.

After failing to cut their way into the van with what is believed to have been a chain saw, some of the gang forced the driver and a guard to open the rear door at gunpoint.

Other members of the gang went along a line of 20 cars which had been forced to stop by the ambush, threatened the drivers and seized their ignition keys which they threw into woodland beside the road.

The robbery, which lasted about 10 minutes began soon after 9 a.m. on the A229 road at Bluebell Hill. The Securicor van, with a crew of four and carrying money to London from its base near Aylesbury, was sandwiched by two vehicles.

One braked in front of the van and, as it slowed, reversed into its bonnet. The other rammed the rear of the van.

"They took a number of bags of cash but left some behind," a Securicor spokesman said.

Van abandoned

The gang escaped in a white Transit van and a green Ford Granada, which they abandoned about a mile away and drove off in at least two other cars, one of them a white Jaguar with a V registration, and possibly a brown Cortina.

The Securicor crew sent out a radio call for help after they were ambushed. Kent police set up roadblocks, but the raiders escaped the net.

Number these events in the order in which they *actually* occurred. If two events occurred at the same time, give them the same number.

One vehicle braked in front of the van and reversed into it. *1*

Some of the gang threatened other drivers and threw away their ignition keys. *5*

The gang stole over £1 million from the van. *6*

The men tried to cut their way into the van. *4*

The gang forced the driver and guard to open the door. *5*

The Securicor van was sandwiched by two cars. *3*

One vehicle rammed the rear of the van. *2*

The gang escaped in a white van and a green car. *7*

The gang drove off in a white Jaguar and a brown Cortina. *10*

Kent police set up roadblocks. *11*

The Securicor crew sent out a call for help. *8*

The gang abandoned the white van and green car. *9*

LANGUAGE SUMMARY

1 Linking words for time relations: narrative

When you are reporting events, the following things can happen:

   (i)   one event can happen *after* another

  (ii) one event can happen *before* another

 (iii) one event can happen *at the same time as* another.

(i) *One event after another* The simplest way of showing that one event occurs after another is to use **and**:

He jumped out of the car **and** rushed to the bank.

If you want to emphasise that the two actions were completely separate, you can use **then** or **after**:

He looked up and down the street. **Then** he went into the bank.

After looking up and down the street, he went into the bank.

If one event follows another very quickly, you can use one of the following expressions:

I came into the room and noticed something was wrong	**at once.** **immediately.**
As soon as **Immediately** **The moment**	I came into the room I noticed something was wrong.

If something happens suddenly or unexpectedly, you can use **suddenly**:

I walked away from the car. **Suddenly** I heard a cry.

If one event occurs some time after another, you can use **later**:

The men drove off in a black car.	The police arrived ten minutes **later.** Ten minutes **later** the police arrived.

(ii) *One event before another*

Before	turning right, he slowed down. he turned right, he slowed down.

11

(iii) *Two simultaneous events* Events can be seen as being 'long' (walking down a street) or 'short' (shutting a door/leaving a room). This distinction can affect the linking words and the verb forms you use.

Two 'short' events can happen simultaneously:

As **Just as**	the men left the bank	the police arrived.

Two 'long' events can happen simultaneously:

While **As**	one man	kept was keeping	watch,	the other	searched for ... was searching for ...
	One man		watch.	**Meanwhile**, the other	searched for... was searching for ...

One or more 'short' events can occur during a long one:

As **While** **When**	we were watching TV	the burglars stole the silver.

2 Using the passive
The passive is often used in reports of events. It can be used for a variety of reasons.

(i) When it is not important who did the action:

> A man found two cars abandoned near Chatham.
> *Two cars were found abandoned near Chatham.*

(ii) When you don't know who did the action:

> Someone stole ten watches from a jeweller's shop last night.
> *Ten watches were stolen from a jeweller's shop last night.*

(iii) To change the focus:

> A giant wave swept a small girl into the sea.
> *A small girl was swept into the sea by a giant wave.*

In the first sentence, the wave is more important; in the second sentence the girl is more important.

Exercise 1
Combining

(i) The following statements were made by witnesses of a bank robbery.
Combine the sentences in each statement using expressions from the language summary.

I was crossing the road. A black car with three men in it came round the corner. It nearly knocked me over.

I saw two men come into the bank. I sounded the alarm.

I saw the car pull up. I knew something was wrong. I ran to phone the police.

Two men got out of the car. They ran into the bank. One man waited behind in the car.

My colleague tried to sound the alarm. They shot him in the arm.

One man came over to the counter. The other stayed near the door.

The car drove off. The police arrived.

The men ran out of the bank. They jumped into the waiting car.

I had just taken some money out of the drawer. I was counting it. I looked up. I saw two men with stockings over their heads.

The man threatened me with a gun. He forced me to give him the money.

(ii) Number the events in the order in which they occurred. Then write a short summary of the robbery.

(iii) Go back to the exercise on the reading passage. Use the numbered sentences to write a short summary of the incident. Combine the sentences using linking words from the language summary.

Exercise 2
Rewriting

(i) Change the verbs in these texts to the passive. How is the effect changed?

> A fire trapped a small girl in an upstairs bedroom last night. Firemen rescued her and an ambulance took her to hospital. She was unhurt, but nurses treated her for shock.

> Thieves stole a hundred watches from a jeweller's shop last night. A man saw a blue van driving away from the shop shortly before someone discovered the theft. I believe the watches to be worth over £10,000.

(ii) Change the passive verbs in these texts to active voice. How is the effect changed?

> A bank was broken into by three armed men carrying machine guns yesterday. Staff and customers were held at gunpoint and over half a million pounds was taken.

> A woman was saved by a schoolboy from drowning last night.

> Four stranded climbers were rescued by helicopter last night.

> Half a million pounds' worth of diamonds were seized by customs officers yesterday.

PARAGRAPH OUTLINE   A newspaper report summarises information gathered from various sources. It may not always report events in the order in which they occurred, but usually starts with an introductory sentence or two, summarising the incident. The rest of the report will go back over the incident in more detail.

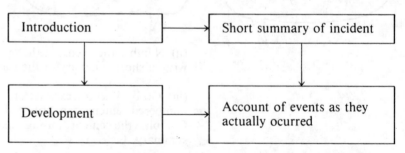

Exercise 3   (i) The sentences in the newspaper report opposite are in muddled
Reordering   order. Number the sentences in the right order. Follow this plan:

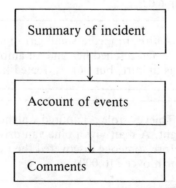

14

Luckily the wave took Lorna to Lena's side — and for 15 minutes she fought to keep her playmate's head above water until the angry seas tore them apart.

Lena Buckingham, a non-swimmer, was knocked unconscious as the wave hit her at Splash Point, Watchet, Somerset.

Daniel, who had been mooring his father's 25ft fishing boat in the harbour, plunged into the sea to grab drowning Lena, then pulled her into the boat.

Her friend Lorna Webber, aged nine, was also carried into the sea as the next wave pounded the harbour wall.

He said at his harbourside home in Mill Lane, Watchet, last night,

"I saw the girl floating face down so I grabbed a lifebuoy and swam to her.

TWO children who saved the life of a 10-year-old girl swept into the sea by a giant wave were recommended for bravery awards by coastguards yesterday.

I managed to get the girl alongside the boat.

Then as Lorna of Portland Terrace, Watchet, struggled ashore, the second hero — 14-year-old Daniel Norman — went into action after hearing cries for help.

I climbed aboard, still hanging on to her, then pulled her in."

Completion   (ii) Write a suitable introductory sentence, summarising the essential facts, for each of these newspaper reports.

a

. . . .
. . . .

The robbers burst into the bank just before it closed at 3.30 p.m. and held three cashiers and four customers at gunpoint for ten minutes. They took over £10,000 and escaped in a blue Ford car. The car was later found abandoned about five miles north of the town.

b

. . . .
. . . .

Sarah, aged three, was found wandering in a North London street yesterday afternoon and taken to Highgate police station. After her picture appeared on the six o'clock news, her mother, Mrs Alice Peters rushed to the police station and mother and daughter were reunited.

c

. . . .
. . . .

Tony was near the top of the mountain when the rope snapped and he fell twenty feet on to a ledge, breaking both legs. He lay there for twelve hours while his companions made the descent to fetch help. He was rescued by a helicopter in the early hours of yesterday morning.

Guided writing   (iii) In a report you may have to collect and organise information from various sources. The comments on the next page are all made by people who witnessed or who were involved in a fire. Follow the suggested outline and use the information in the comments to write a newspaper report about the incident.

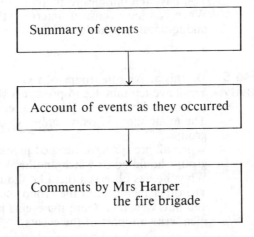

| Summary of events |
| Account of events as they occurred |
| Comments by Mrs Harper / the fire brigade |

We think the fire must have been started by a cigarette.

Official Comment Fire Brigade.

We got the fire under control fairly easily and were able to put it out within half an hour. As soon as the smoke and flames were under control I ran into the house to see if there was anyone trapped in the upstairs rooms and I found an old lady still asleep in bed!

Tony Owen Fireman.

I was about to go to bed when there was a frantic knocking at the door. I opened the door and found Mr Peters who told me about the fire and asked to use my phone. While he rang the fire brigade, I woke up my family and some neighbours. We organised a team of helpers and attempted to put the fire out, using hoses and buckets.

Tom Stewart Neighbour of Mrs Harper.

This has all come as such a shock! I had no idea that the fire had started, and was very surprised when the firemen woke me up. I'm upset about the damage, of course, — but really I'm just thankful to be alive.

Mrs Anne Harper Widow, aged 80.

It was about 11 o'clock and I was coming back from the pub when I noticed smoke and flames coming from the ground floor of the house on the corner of Grace Street and Prince's Avenue. I immediately ran to the nearest house and asked if I could use their phone.

John Peters 18-year-old law student.

Exercise 4 Free writing	Do this activity in groups of four.

**Exercise 4
Free writing**

Do this activity in groups of four.
Each group should split into two pairs and prepare the following stories:

A + B: You were in a plane when it was hijacked!
C + D: You were kidnapped!

Talk to your partner and decide what happened.
You have ten minutes to prepare your story.
When you have finished, interview the other pair in your group, taking notes as you do so, and then write a report.

**Exercise 5
Writing activity**

Do this activity in groups of six.
You have ten minutes to prepare a short mime of an exciting event (a bank robbery ... a fire ... a terrorist attack ... a rescue ...). The mime should involve only five out of the six members of your group.
When all groups have finished preparing, one person from each group should go to watch another group's mime.
When he has observed them he should return to his own group.
The other members of the group should act as a team of reporters and interview him about the events he witnessed. Take notes and then write a report of the events.

Unit 3 Complaints

Organising an argument: justification

Reading Read the letters and then do the activity on the next page in pairs.

A

24 Park Road,
Guildford.

6 July 1982

Dear Sir,
I am writing to you in connection with a
pair of shoes from your Sunny Wave range,
which I purchased in May from Cloggs, High
Street, Leatherhead.
The manager of Cloggs specially
recommended these shoes for sailing, as they
had non-slip soles and were resistant to salt
water. I have only worn these shoes for their
intended purpose, sailing, on seven occasions,
yet, as you will see the non-slip soles have
worn completely smooth. Further, when purchased
the shoes were a deep navy-blue colour, but now
they have a faded, shabby appearance.
I enclose the receipt for £20 and would
appreciate a refund or replacement pair of
higher quality.
Yours faithfully,

F. L. Gardener

B

Dear Mrs Johnson,
I feel I must protest about your
behaviour, although I have borne it in
patience for the last two months since
you moved in.
I am constantly disturbed by noise
from your record player late at night.
I have spoken to you a number of
times about this matter and you did
say you would try to be more reasonable.
Furthermore, your dogs are causing us
a good deal of annoyance - their
constant barking is very disturbing.
As you know, my wife is a nurse and
is frequently on night duty, so she
needs to have peace and quiet during
the day.
I hope we can manage to sort this out
amicably.
Yours,
James Gratton

C

5 Rose Street,
Cardiff.

5 November 1982

Dear Sir,

I am writing to you about a raincoat
that I purchased last month from your shop
in Charles Street.

Although I was assured by your manager
that the coat was fully waterproof, I was
soaked to the skin the first time that I
wore it in the rain. In addition, the
stitching on the seams is already beginning
to come undone.

I enclose the receipt for £50 and
would be grateful for a refund.

Yours faithfully,

M. Birtwhistle (Mrs)

D

6 Green Lane,
Newton Abbot.

12 April 1982

Dear Sir,
I am writing to you regarding a fridge that
I purchased in February from your branch in South
Street, Exeter.
The fridge was one of the more expensive
models in the Electro range and is fully
guaranteed for a year. Despite the fact that I
have only had the fridge for two months, the
thermostat has now broken. Moreover, the
interior is so badly designed that the salad
compartment broke in the first week.
I enclose the receipt for £300 and would be
grateful for replacement or repair under the
terms of the guarantee.
Yours faithfully,

J. Simpson

(i) Read letter A. Imagine that one of you is Mrs Gardener. The other is the shop assistant in Cloggs. Mrs Gardener has just brought the shoes back to complain about them. Act out the conversation.

(ii) Read letter B. One of you is Mr Gratton. You are telling your friend about your problem neighbour. Act out the conversation.

(iii) Read letter C. One of you is the shop assistant. The other is the manager. Mrs Birtwhistle has just brought her raincoat back to the shop. The assistant sees the manager and explains to him what has happened. Act out the conversation.

(iv) Read letter D. One of you is Mr Simpson. Complain to your friend about your new fridge. Act out the conversation.

LANGUAGE SUMMARY   *1 Expressing complaints*
Letters of complaint are usually formal and dignified in tone.
The first sentence of a letter usually states the subject of the complaint.
This complaint can be *mild* or *strong*.

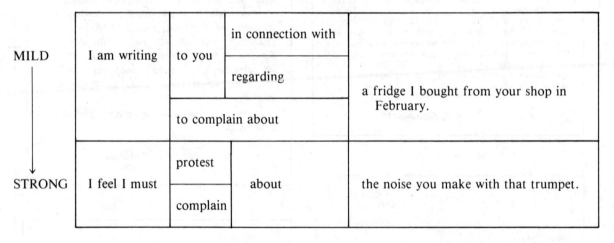

MILD	I am writing	to you	in connection with	a fridge I bought from your shop in February.
			regarding	
		to complain about		
STRONG	I feel I must	protest	about	the noise you make with that trumpet.
		complain		

Letters of complaint usually end with a request or a suggestion.
The following table summarises some ways of ending letters of complaint.

I hope	we can sort this out amicably.
	this situation will not occur again.
I trust	
I would be grateful if	you would send me a refund.
I would appreciate	a refund.

2 Linking words for justification

When we make a complaint, we usually *justify* it, ie state our reasons for complaining. The justification can precede or follow the complaint.

COMPLAINT		JUSTIFICATION	COMPLAINT
The shoes are completely worn out	**although** **even though** **despite the fact that** **in spite of the fact that**	I've only worn them six times.	
	Although **Even though** **Desite the fact that** **In spite of the fact that**	I've only worn them six times,	the shoes are completely worn out.
		I've only worn these shoes six times	**but** **. Despite this** **. Nevertheless**	they are completely worn out.

*(Note: bottom section — I've only worn these shoes six times / **but** · **Despite this** · **Nevertheless** / they are completely worn out.)*

Exercise 1
Matching

Match justification and complaint and join them with a linking word from the language summary.

Justification

I have only worn the shoes three times

you said it was suitable for children

I washed it very carefully

you promised to clean it with care

I've written three times

I sent you a cheque three months ago

I followed the instructions very carefully

I have asked you repeatedly not to lean your bicycle against my shop window

Complaint

my new dress is ruined

the book is disgusting

you still keep sending me the same telephone bill

it shrank

it broke the first time I used it

you still haven't repaired the dial

you persist in doing so

the soles are worn out already

Exercise 2
Completion

Write a beginning and an end for these letters. Use expressions from language summary 1.

(i)

....
Although I have spoken to you a number of times and you promised to repair the fence between our gardens, it is still broken. Your dogs continue to come into our garden and are causing us a good deal of annoyance. ....
....

(ii)

....
Even though I have only worn the dress three times, the seams are already beginning to come undone. ....
....

(iii)

....
I followed the manufacturer's instructions very carefully but the blender broke the first time I used it. ....
....

(iv)

....
You continue to park your car in an unauthorised area despite the fact that you have been repeatedly asked not to do so.
....

(v)

....
I have spoken to you a number of times about noise and asked you to be more considerate. In spite of this, you continue to play your record player till the early hours of the morning.
....

General and collective nouns

(i) Look at these sentences.

I would be grateful if you could repair the $\boxed{\text{car}}$ or exchange it for a better made $\boxed{\text{car}}$.

I would be grateful if you would repair the $\boxed{\text{car}}$ or exchange it for a better made $\boxed{\text{model}}$.

You can avoid repetition either by using a general term:

Car	—	model
Shirt	—	garment
Dishwasher	—	machine

Or by using a collective noun:

Shoes	—	pair
Teacups	—	set

(ii) Choose a word from this list to fill in the blanks in the sentences below.

model   set   pair   machine   garment   box

1 These chocolates were stale. I would appreciate another . . . .
2 These knives are discoloured. I would appreciate a new . . . .
3 This radio is unsatisfactory. I would be grateful if you would send me a new . . . .
4 These socks are too big. I wonder if you could replace them with a new . . . .
5 This lawn mower doesn't work. I would appreciate a replacement . . . .
6 This jumper is rather faded in appearance. I would appreciate replacement with a . . . . . . of higher quality.

PARAGRAPH OUTLINE   The letters in the reading passage were organised like this:

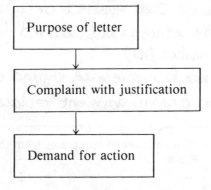

Purpose of letter

↓

Complaint with justification

↓

Demand for action

(i) The following letter is in muddled order. Use the paragraph
outline to help you rewrite it in a more logical order.

Dear Sir,

I have only done 500 miles since buying the car, but already several
problems have arisen.

I am writing to you regarding my car, a silver-blue Astral, purchased
ten days ago from your garage.

Further, several smaller details are highly unsatisfactory.

In particular, the engine is extremely noisy and the acceleration is
poor, especially on hills.

I would be grateful if you would repair the car as quickly as possible,
under the terms of the guarantee, or exchange it for a better-made model.

The boot lid will not lock, the car radio does not work properly and the
seat belts are jammed.

The oil consumption also seems to be rather high.

                    Yours faithfully,

                    R A Wheale

                    R. A. Wheale

Guided writing   (ii) Read this complaint form:

Form xrb/1198QS

Item:	Pullover
Range:	Autumn Gold
Date of purchase:	June 8th 1983
Where purchased:	Ribbons Boutique, Fore Street, Chesham
Details of complaint:	Manager specially recommended it as guaranteed against shrinking and fading. Has only been washed once yet shrunk to ½ size. When purchased was deep red. Now faded pink colour.
Receipt:	Enclosed (value £10)
Comments:	Customer would appreciate refund or replacement.
Action:	If customer returns garment replacement will be sent.

Write a letter of complaint from the customer to the manager of
Ribbons.

Exercise 4
Free writing

Do this activity in pairs.
First, go back to Exercise 1 and choose one of the situations. Then improvise a dialogue between the people in the situation (neighbour/neighbour, customer/shop assistant).
When you have finished, write a letter of complaint.

Exercise 5
Writing activity

Do this activity in groups of four.
Divide your group into two pairs.
Each pair should improvise the following situation:

> You live either side of a common neighbour. Recently her behaviour has been annoying you. Discuss her behaviour and say what annoys you.

Now change partners.
Improvise the following situation:

> You meet each other in the street and stop to talk. Complain about your neighbours!

Now write a letter to your neighbour. You have had enough of the situation and want to put an end to it!

Unit 4 Telling a story

Pace, suspense and variety in a narrative

Reading The following short story is a simplified and condensed version of a story by Saki, a famous early twentieth-century short story writer. Read the story and do the exercise which follows.

The disappearance of Crispina Umberleigh

In the first-class carriage of a train travelling across the Hungarian plain towards Yugoslavia, two British middle-aged men sat engaged in friendly conversation. They had first met on boarding the train at the German border and after a day's break of journey in Vienna, they had met again on the station platform and chosen to sit together again. The elder of the two looked and behaved like a diplomat: he was in fact a wine merchant. The other was certainly a journalist. Neither man was talkative, and each was grateful to the other for not talking too much. That is why, from time to time, they talked.

In Vienna, on the previous day, they had heard about the theft of a famous painting from the Louvre, and so the topic of their conversation was mysterious disappearances.

'Did you ever hear about the famous case of my aunt, Crispina Umberleigh?' asked the wine merchant.

'I remember hearing about it, yes,' said the journalist, 'but I never knew exactly what happened.'

'Well, to begin with, I must say that the family were not exactly unhappy about Crispina's disappearance. She was one of those people born to organise and to command. Her sons and daughters were terrified of her; their studies, friendships, diet and amusements were all controlled by their mother. Her husband lived in terror of her. So everyone was amazed when, one day, she suddenly and inexplicably vanished. It was as if St Paul's Cathedral or the Houses of Parliament had disappeared overnight, leaving nothing but an open space.'

'What was the effect on the family?' asked the journalist.

'All the girls bought themselves bicycles and started smoking cigarettes. Meanwhile, the boys put forward a theory that their mother had gone abroad, and went to France to look for her. Actually, they spent most of their time in certain districts of Paris where they were most unlikely to find her.'

'And couldn't your uncle find any clues?' asked the journalist.

'In fact he received a message a few days after she left. The message said that his wife had been kidnapped, and

---

was being kept on a small island off the coast of Norway. She was living in comfort and being well cared for. With the information came a demand for money: a lump sum, and £2000 per year. If the kidnappers did not receive the money, they would send her back immediately!'

The journalist began to laugh. 'What did your uncle do?' he asked.

'Well, he is a kind old man and a considerate father, so he paid the lump sum at once, and continued to pay £2000 a year to the kidnappers for eight years. Every year he received a report on her health from them.'

'What did the police do meanwhile?' asked the journalist.

'They continued to look for Crispina, and from time to time they came to report to my uncle, but of course he never told them anything about his arrangement with the kidnappers. Then, after an absence of more than eight years, Crispina suddenly returned.'

'Had she escaped from the kidnappers?'

'She had never been kidnapped. Her disappearance had been caused by a complete loss of memory. She had wandered as far as Birmingham, and found employment there. Then suddenly, after eight years, her memory returned, and she found her way back home.'

'What about the kidnappers ...?'

'They had invented the whole story. It was a clever trick to get some money from my uncle. A butler had heard of Crispina's disappearance, and taken advantage of the situation. Crispina, although she was back home, never regained control over her children. They had enjoyed their freedom for eight years and could not be brought back under her strict discipline. Her husband ended a broken man. The strain of explaining how he had spent £16,000 in the last eight years was too much for him.... But here we are at Belgrade, and I must leave you. Goodbye.'

Number these events in the order in which they actually happened. (If two events happened at the same time, give them the same number.)

The train arrived at Belgrade.
The wine merchant and the journalist met first in Germany.
They spent one day in Vienna.
The wine merchant told the journalist a story.
The wine merchant and the journalist were sitting in a train carriage.
Crispina disappeared.
Mr Umberleigh received a letter from some kidnappers.
The police searched for Crispina.
Crispina returned home.
Mr Umberleigh paid out £16,000 over eight years.
Crispina lost her memory.
Crispina's memory returned.
The girls started smoking and riding bicycles.
The boys went to Europe.
Crispina worked in Birmingham.

LANGUAGE SUMMARY Look at the language summary in Unit 2. All the language there can be useful in a story as well as in a report. This unit will practise ways of *organising narrative*.

Most stories narrate a sequence of events. These events are not always narrated in the order in which they occurred. The following things can happen:

(i) The narrator can narrate the events in order, like this:

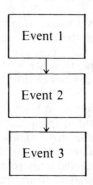

(ii) The narrator can leave a long interval of time between one section of the narrative and the next, like this:

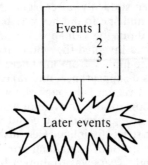

(iii) The narrator can narrate simultaneously what was happening to two different people or in two different places, like this:

Place/Person A   Place/Person B

Event

	1		1
	2		2
	3		3

(iv) The narrator can tell us about an event that happened before the story began, like this:

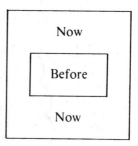

This technique is called *flashback*.

Exercise 1
Plot

Look at the Saki story. The time scheme is very complicated. Try to draw a diagram!

Now read the outlines on the following pages, for stories which all happen on trains: How do they correspond to the four outlines given above?

a

Jane is waiting on the platform.

↓

She buys a paper to read on the train.

↓

The train comes in.

↓

She gets in and sits opposite a man in an otherwise empty carriage.

↓

She picks up the paper.

↓

The man leans forward and starts talking.

↓

They talk for about thirty minutes.

↓

The train reaches the next station.

↓

The man gets out.

↓

The train leaves.

↓

She unfolds her paper. On the front page is a picture of the man she has been talking to, under the headline: *Police Hunt Escaped Murderer.*

b

You are on holiday in Cornwall.

You catch a train to Penzance.

The train stops in a small place called Barcombe.

Everyone gets out.

A porter tells you that this is the terminus.

You realise that you have caught the wrong train.

You get out.

You find that there isn't a train back till the next day.

You spend the day and night in Barcombe and have a wonderful time.

It is a charming, pretty place.

... Twenty years later you are back in Cornwall.

You decide to go back to Barcombe.

You go to the station but no one has ever heard of the place.

You look on a map but can't find it.

No one you meet has ever heard of the place!

c

It is war time. Suzanne, who works for an underground organisation, has been given some important papers to deliver to a contact in another town. She ties her hair in long plaits in order to look younger, and puts the papers in a school satchel.

She catches the train.

On the train she falls asleep, using the satchel as a pillow.

The train is searched by the military police. The old lady opposite prevents them from waking Suzanne by saying 'Look, she's only a schoolgirl, let her sleep!'

Suzanne wakes up and gets off the train. She will never know what happened.

d

Start here

Anna is waiting on the station platform. She has returned from a year abroad and is on her way to see her fiancé, Rob.	Rob is eating breakfast in the front room in his flat. He is reading Anna's last letter and has her photo propped up on the coffee pot in front of him ... He gets up and clears away.
Anna has got on the train and sat down opposite a young man in jeans and a blue tee-shirt. The train moves off. The young man offers her a cigarette.	Rob has finished washing up and puts his jacket on. He gets his car keys and drives to the station.
Anna and the young man are deep in conversation. She has told him about Rob and how worried she is about the reunion.	Rob has found he's far too early for the train and has gone for a coffee. He has sat down opposite a young woman in jeans and a blue tee-shirt. They start talking and he begins to tell her about Anna.
The train is pulling into the station. The young man asks for Anna's phone number. She gives it to him.	The girl and Rob have got up and are standing on the platform. He asks for her phone number. She gives it to him.
Anna gets off the train.	The girl gets on.

e

A train pulls into the station. You look out and see a train on
the opposite platform. One of the passengers in the train
looks familiar. You realise it's Bob Randall — you knew him
at school.

You were rivals at school.
In your last term at school, you were involved
with a group of boys who went into shops and
stole things. You never actually stole things
yourself, but were friends with one of the boys
who did. Somehow the headmaster found out
about the stealing, and *you* were expelled from
the school. You don't know who told him, but
you always suspected Bob. You refused to talk
to him again, and shortly afterwards he left
town, so you never saw him again.

The train begins to move. The man turns his head and sees
you. He stands up, and pulls down the window. As the train
leaves the station, he shouts, 'You're wrong. It was all a
mistake.'

Exercise 2
Suspense

When you are telling a story, you have to make the reader want to
know what is going to happen next. You have to create suspense.
Here are some ways to do this:

1   Create a mystery. Don't explain it till the end.

2   Give the story a surprise ending. Give some hints that something
    unusual is going to happen.

3   Include some unexpected events during the story.

(i) How does Saki create suspense?

What is the mystery in the story?

What is the surprise at the end?

Did anything unexpected happen in the middle of the story?

(ii) Look at outlines **a** and **b**.

These stories have surprise endings.

Choose one and write it.

Think how you could   a) include some hints that something
                          unusual is going to happen
              or   b) include some unexpected events.

I.A.L.S. BOOKSTORE

Exercise 3
Variety

When you are telling a story you have to keep the reader's interest. You have to create variety. Here are some ways to do this:

1 You can change the scene.

2 You can move back or forward in time.

3 You can move from one group of characters to another.

(i) Look at the Saki story.
Where are the changes of scene?
Where does it move back and forward in time?
Where does it move from one group of characters to another?

(ii) Look at outlines **c**, **d** and **e**.
How do they create variety? Choose one of the outlines and write the story.

Exercise 4
Pace

Finally, you have to vary the pace of your story. Here are some ways to do this:

1 You can use a mixture of long and short sentences. Too many long sentences may make your story monotonous. Too many short sentences make it very jerky. You can use short sentences to create an effect of surprise or to signal a change in your narrative.

2 You can include some dialogue in your story. This changes the pace and makes the story livelier.

(i) Look at the Saki story.
What would the effect of the first paragraph be if it read like this?

> A train was travelling across the Hungarian plain towards Yugoslavia. Two men sat in the first-class carriage. They had met in Germany. They had spent a day in Vienna. They had met again on the station platform. They had chosen to sit together again.

What would the effect of the second to last paragraph be if it read like this?

> It appeared that she had never in fact been kidnapped, but had wandered as far as Birmingham, remaining there and working for eight years until her memory returned and she found her way back home.

How would the effect be changed if the journalist's questions were omitted and the story were told as a continuous narrative?

(ii) Go back and look at the stories you have written. Could you rewrite any parts of them to make them livelier and to change the pace?

Exercise 5
Free writing

Write your own train story:
Give your story a surprise ending or begin with a mystery.
Include a flashback or a change of scene.
Include some dialogue.
Vary the length of your sentences.

Unit 5 Police reports

Reporting events

Explaining cause and effect

Reading Read the legal plaint describing a road accident, and do the exercises which follow. The glossary will help you to understand any difficult vocabulary.

IN THE BRACKNELL COUNTY COURT   Plaint No. 79/123.

BETWEEN:

FREDERICK GARDENER   PLAINTIFF
— and —
ARTHUR ROADHOG   DEFENDANT

PARTICULARS OF CLAIM

1. On or about Saturday, the 11th day of August, the Plaintiff was crossing on foot High Street, Bracknell, from the East side to the West side at or near the junction of such road with Broad Lane when a collision occurred between a wheelbarrow being pushed by the Plaintiff and a motor car, registration number HOG 1, then being driven by the Defendant along High Street, travelling North in the direction of Slough.

2. The said accident was caused by the negligence of the Defendant.

PARTICULARS

(1)   The Defendant was negligent in that he
  (i)   failed to obey a traffic signal
  (ii)   failed to observe and/or heed the presence of the Plaintiff
  (iii)   failed to give the Plaintiff passage
  (iv)   failed to keep any or any proper look-out
  (v)   drove too fast
  (vi)   failed so to stop slow down or turn aside so as to avoid the said collision.

(2)   The Defendant's negligence caused the Plaintiff to suffer personal injury, loss and damage.

(A)   *Personal Injury* As a result of the accident the Plaintiff suffered contusions and abrasions of the buttocks, necessitating suturing, and resulting in severe pain, suffering and embarrassment to the Plaintiff over a period of four weeks.

(B) *Destruction of Marrow* The Wheelbarrow referred to in paragraph 1 hereof contained a vegetable marrow which was of extraordinary size and quality, being approximately 65 lb in weight. The said marrow was destroyed in the collision. Consequently, it was deprived of the opportunity of winning the County Show Annual Vegetable Marrow Championship, which would have substantially enhanced its value and the Plaintiff's reputation as a grower of outstanding vegetable marrow. In addition the Plaintiff was deprived of the valuable breeding potential of the said marrow.

(C)	Special Damage	£
(i)	Loss of earnings for two weeks @ £50 per week	100.00
(ii)	One 'Workhorse' Wheelbarrow	18.00
(iii)	Damage to clothing	24.00
(iv)	Admission Ticket to County Show	3.00
(v)	Entry Fee for Vegetable Marrow Championship	0.50
		145.50

WHEREFORE the Plaintiff claims DAMAGES.

Dated this 8th Day of October 1982

Good & Honest of
2 High Street, Bracknell.

Solicitors for the Plaintiff

To: The Registrar and the Defendant

Glossary
said the event/person/object previously mentioned
defendant the person who is accused
plaintiff the person who is complaining
negligence carelessness
heed attention
further in addition
conviction the act of finding someone guilty
liability responsibility in law
contusions bruises
abrasions cuts
suturing stitches
enhance increase
wherefore for these reasons
in that because
marrow a large green vegetable
potential ability
breed grow new plants
necessity need
passage room to pass by
road hog a person who behaves as if he is the only person on the road

(i) *Where it happened.* Draw a map of the junction between High Street and Board Lane in the space below. Label Slough/the site of the accident/the traffic lights/North.

(ii) *Who did what?* Draw a line to connect these events with the person who did them. Then number the events in the order in which they happened.

GARDENER

DROVE THROUGH A RED LIGHT
HAD GROWN A PRIZE MARROW
KNOCKED GARDENER OVER
WAS CROSSING THE HIGH STREET   ROADHOG
WAS TAKING HIS MARROW TO THE COUNTY SHOW
COLLIDED WITH THE WHEELBARROW
OVERTURNED THE WHEELBARROW
DESTROYED THE MARROW

(iii) *Who said what?* Write *Gardener* or *Roadhog* by the sentences to identify the speaker and then reorder the sentences to make a dialogue.
Invent some more remarks and add them to the dialogue.

_____	You old fool! Why don't you look before you cross the road?
_____	You were driving much too fast.
_____	Didn't you hear when I hooted?
_____	You must be blind! Didn't you see me coming?
_____	Oh no! All that work for nothing!
_____	And my trousers are torn!
_____	That barrow cost me £18!
_____	This is a road, not a farmyard!
_____	Didn't you see the lights were red?
_____	Who cares about the marrow? Look at the damage to my Mercedes.
_____	And this is Bracknell High Street, not a motorway!
_____	The front bumper's buckled and the headlights are smashed.
_____	That's at least £300 worth of repairs.
_____	Now I haven't a hope of winning the Show.

LANGUAGE SUMMARY When you are writing eye-witness reports you will have to do two things:

1 describe the scene or situation leading up to the incident that took place (briefly and factually)

2 report the events that took place.

The tables below summarise describing a situation and reporting events.

1 Describing situations leading up to an incident

Situation that is going on	The car was pulling out from the kerb I was going to the bank		
Situation that has been going on for a long time	The blue car had been waiting for ten minutes I had been sitting on the wall for some time	**when**	the accident occurred.
Situation that has just finished	I had just come out of the shop The blue car had just arrived		
Situation about to happen at time of event	I was about to cross the road The blue car was about to start		

When you are describing a series of actions, you may have to explain why something happened, or show how one action led to another.
The following tables summarise some linking words for *cause and effect*.

2 Linking words for cause and effect
You can show that an event was caused by certain conditions or actions by using *as a result*, *consequently* or *so*:

CAUSE		EFFECT
The roads were icy He was driving much too fast The driver lost control	.*As a result .*Consequently so	he skidded. he couldn't stop in time. the car crashed into a wall.

These expressions are more formal, and would only be used in writing.

If an action has an effect on *someone* or *something else*, you can use a verb like *cause* or *make*:

CAUSE		EFFECT
The red car hit the blue car	. *This caused *causing	it to swerve.
	. This made making	it swerve.

If an action and its result happen *in the same instant*, you can use a present participle:

CAUSE	EFFECT
He collided with the bicycle,	**overturning** it. **injuring** the cyclist. **damaging** it badly.

These expressions are more formal, and would only be used in writing.

Exercise 1
Free writing

These people all witnessed a road accident:

Imagine you are each of the people in the picture opposite in turn. Write a sentence describing what you had just done, were doing or were about to do when the accident happened.

Exercise 2
Combining

The witnesses of the accident all gave different accounts of what occurred. Below are extracts from the statements they made to the police describing what they saw. Combine the sentences, using a linking word from the language summary.

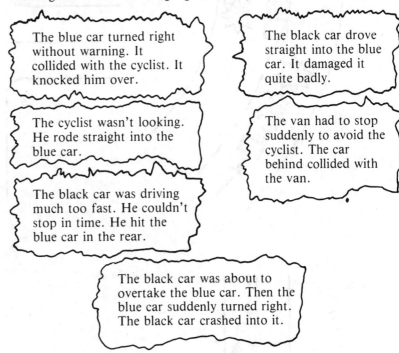

The blue car turned right without warning. It collided with the cyclist. It knocked him over.

The black car drove straight into the blue car. It damaged it quite badly.

The cyclist wasn't looking. He rode straight into the blue car.

The van had to stop suddenly to avoid the cyclist. The car behind collided with the van.

The black car was driving much too fast. He couldn't stop in time. He hit the blue car in the rear.

The black car was about to overtake the blue car. Then the blue car suddenly turned right. The black car crashed into it.

PARAGRAPH OUTLINE

You can organise an eye-witness report or police statement like this:

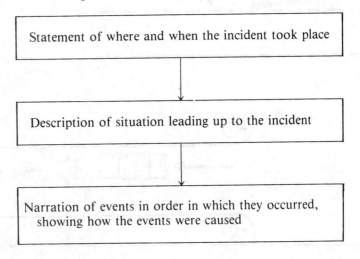

Statement of where and when the incident took place

Description of situation leading up to the incident

Narration of events in order in which they occurred, showing how the events were caused

Exercise 3
Guided writing

Describe the situations leading up to each of the incidents below and then describe how the accidents occurred.

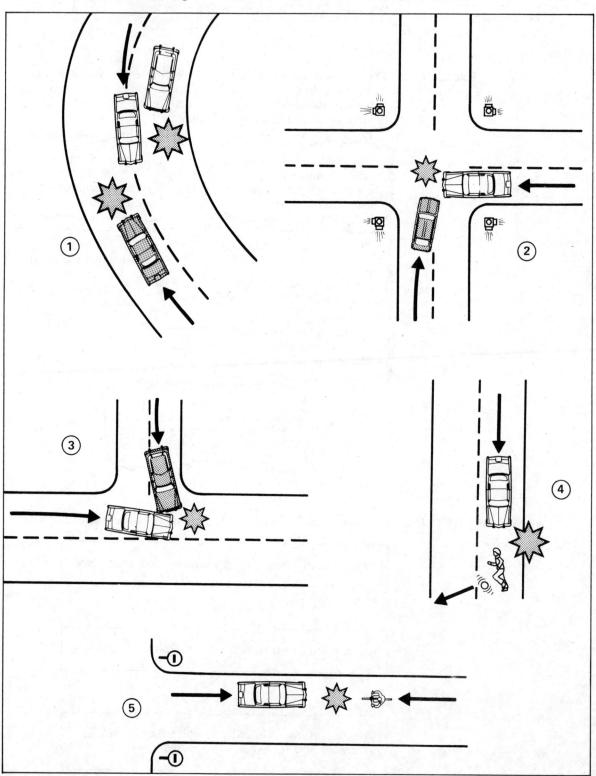

38

Exercise 4
Free writing

Do this activity in pairs.

Improvise the argument between Gardener and Roadhog at the scene of the accident.

Each of you should try to blame the other for the accident.

When you have finished arguing, write a letter to your solicitor to claim compensation for the accident. State where and when the accident took place, and describe how it happened. Show that it was not your fault!

Begin like this:

Dear Sir,
I am writing to report an accident that occurred ...
and end like this;
I would therefore like to claim damages for injury and damage sustained in the accident.

Exercise 5
Writing activity

Do this activity in groups of six.

Read the background information first:

There has been an accident at the junction of Hedge Lane and East Street. You were all involved in the accident — as drivers, passengers, witnesses or policemen.

Student A should look at Activity A on page 126
　　　　B　　 "　　　"　　"　　" 　F 　"　　"　127
　　　　C　　 "　　　"　　"　　" 　J 　"　　"　129
　　　　D　　 "　　　"　　"　　" 　O 　"　　"　131
　　　　E　　 "　　　"　　"　　" 　R 　"　　"　132
　　　　F　　 "　　　"　　"　　" 　U 　"　　"　134

You have five minutes to look at your card and to memorise the facts.

Then close your books and act out the discussion at the scene of the accident.

When the 'policeman' arrives, tell him everything you saw.

When you have finished, write out a statement for the police, while the policeman writes his own report of the accident.

Unit 6 Pen portraits

Describing appearance and behaviour

Reading   (i) Read the following descriptions and match them to the pictures:

> She was a small, thin girl with long fair hair, a round face and large, round, blue eyes, which gave her a perpetually surprised expression. Her upturned nose and freckles made her look much younger than she actually was. She was always casually dressed, in faded jeans and a tee-shirt.
>
> She was a slim young woman of medium height, with wavy, shoulder-length blonde hair. She had an oval face with a pale complexion, a small, straight nose, firm chin and decided mouth. Elegantly dressed in a tailored suit, she looked determined and efficient.
>
> He was a tall, thin man with receding black hair, bushy eyebrows and a walrus moustache which gave him a fierce expression. He was untidily dressed in an old jacket and cord trousers.
>
> He was a trim, energetic young man with dark, curly hair, brown eyes and a thin moustache. He was neatly dressed in a suit and tie.

(ii) The four descriptions below are all continuations of the four descriptions that you have just read. Match the descriptions below with the pictures and descriptions in (i) opposite.

She walked briskly and with a sense of purpose. When she entered a room, people would stop talking and turn to look at her. She was never late, never forgot a birthday, or missed an appointment.

He had a rather abrupt manner, and would fire questions at you impatiently and often without waiting for an answer. He was rather absent-minded, was always forgetting people's names, leaving his umbrella on trains, or losing his wallet.

She was always cheerful and smiling, and had a habit of giggling at the most unexpected things and at the most unexpected times. She saw life as a joke and people as curiosities.

He was extremely well mannered and very punctual. He always used to write down his appointments in a little leather diary, and kept his desk very tidy. He drank a little, never too much, and never smoked.

LANGUAGE SUMMARY

1 Describing people: appearance and behaviour
When you are describing a person, you may want to include a *description of their appearance* and a *description of their habits and behaviour* as well as an analysis of their characteristics.
The following tables summarise ways of describing *appearance* and *behaviour*.
(i) Describing appearance

Size	He She	was	a tall/small man/woman. of medium height.
Shape	She He		was slim/fat. had a slim figure.
Features and hair	She He		was brown eyed/blonde haired. had brown eyes/blonde hair.
Clothes	She He		was smartly dressed/untidily dressed. wore smart clothes/old clothes. was dressed in a tee-shirt and jeans.
Expression	She He		looked shy/happy. appeared shy/happy. had a a shy/happy expression. was a shy-looking man/woman. had an air of timidity.

(ii) Describing behaviour

She He	always/often/sometimes/never		bit her/his nails.
	would	often/sometimes/always/never	bite her/his nails.
	always often sometimes never	used to	
	When she/he was nervous she/he would		

She He	had a habit of was always	biting her/his nails.

2 Linking words for description

When you are writing a description, you can use a variety of ways to link your sentences together. The following table summarises some ways of linking sentences in description.

(i) You can use **with, which** or **who**.

She was a small, thin, dark woman She had a round face	**with**	rosy cheeks and a cheerful expression. blue eyes and freckles.

She had long blonde hair	**which**	hung down to her shoulders.
He had round eyes		gave him a surprised expression.

He was a small, fierce man She was a small, blonde woman	**who**	was always shouting. wore expensive clothes.

(ii) You can place the adjectives at the beginning of the sentence:

Tall, slim and well dressed, he had an air of brisk efficiency.

(iii) You can use **and, or** or just use commas.

> She was never late, never forgot a birthday **and** never missed an appointment.
> She was never late, never forgot a birthday **or** missed an appointment.
> She was never late, never forgot a birthday, never missed an appointment.

Exercise 1
Completion

Choose suitable words to fill in the blanks.

1   He was a .... slim, ... eyed man with a .... nose and a .... complexion.

2   She was ...., and .... dressed, with ...., ... hair and .... cheeks.

3   She had a .... face, ... hair, ... eyes and a .... complexion.

4   Tall, ..., and .... dressed, he had .... hair, ... eyes, a .... nose and ....

5   Mr Pocock was a .... portly gentleman with a .... a .... and a ...., on his face.

Exercise 2
Combining

Rewrite these descriptions using fewer, longer sentences.

1   He was an old man. He had grey hair. He had a long beard. He wore dark, horn-rimmed glasses. He looked very serious.

2   She was a slim, blonde woman. She had blue eyes. She walked upright. She carried her head high. She appeared taller than she was.

3   Ann's father was a plump gentleman. He looked kindly. He was old. He had a walrus moustache. He wore a tweed jacket. It smelt of tobacco. He used to get up early, before anyone else. He used to smoke a pipe in the garden before breakfast.

4   Jean Buchan was thin. She always looked anxious. She had grey hair. It was tied in a bun. She was always in a hurry. She spoke in short sentences. She did everything at top speed.

5   Just seeing him made you feel happy. He was always laughing. He had a smile and a joke for everyone. His eyes were blue and twinkling. His face was wrinkled. He had leathery skin. He wore faded blue dungarees. He would whistle as he walked down the lane. He would stop to talk to everyone he met.

PARAGRAPH OUTLINE   To make your description come alive for your reader, you should make him feel that he is getting to know the character you are describing. You can do this by making your description move from first impressions to more detailed knowledge of the character, like this:

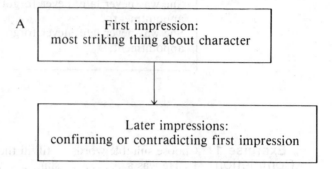

or by making your description move from broad outlines to finer details, like this:

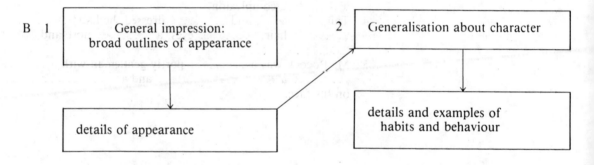

Exercise 3   (i) The following paragraph is in muddled order. Use paragraph
Reordering   outline A to rewrite it in a better order.

She was a strict vegetarian, teetotaller and non-smoker.
We started talking after she had tripped over my suitcase and spilt her coffee all over the book I was reading.
Her appearance, too, was odd and awkward.
However, as you got to know her better, you found that under the eccentricity and shyness was a mind with strong principles and fixed ideas.
She was one of the clumsiest people I had ever met.
I later found that she was disaster-prone.
I first met Alice on a train to Newcastle.
She was always bumping into and falling over things, cutting her fingers, burning or scalding herself in the kitchen.
She was a tall, lanky girl with long black hair, a square face, glasses, and clothes that never seemed to fit properly — usually too large and always the wrong colour.

Guided writing (ii) Use the suggested outline to write a description following paragraph outline B.

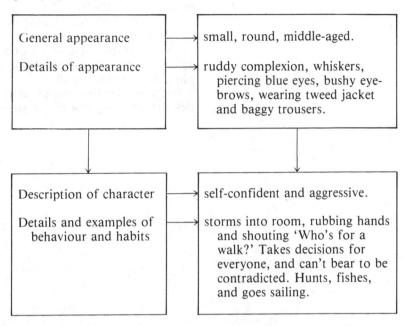

General appearance	→ small, round, middle-aged.
Details of appearance	→ ruddy complexion, whiskers, piercing blue eyes, bushy eyebrows, wearing tweed jacket and baggy trousers.
Description of character	→ self-confident and aggressive.
Details and examples of behaviour and habits	→ storms into room, rubbing hands and shouting 'Who's for a walk?' Takes decisions for everyone, and can't bear to be contradicted. Hunts, fishes, and goes sailing.

Exercise 4 Look at the pictures above. Consider the following questions.
Free writing Discuss them with a partner.

What do the people look like?
How are they dressed?
How would you describe their facial expression?
What are they thinking/feeling?
What do you think they are like? How would they talk/behave?
What are their habits?

Now choose one of the pictures and write about the person.

Exercise 5
Writing activity

(i) Write a description of the person sitting next to you but do not mention his/her name. When you have finished, pin your description to the wall. Then walk round and read all the descriptions. Can you identify everyone?

(ii) Write a short description of a famous person (film star, singer, actor, TV personality, politician, etc). Include a description of his physical appearance and habits but do not mention him by name. When you have finished, get into groups of six. Read your description to the rest of the group. Can they guess who it is?

Unit 7 Advice

Asking for and giving advice

Organising argument: giving reasons

Reading Do this activity in pairs. First, read letters **a** and **b** and then discuss them with your partner. What advice would you offer the writer? Read letters **c** and **d**. Discuss them with your partner. What do you think the original problem was?

a

1 Rose Street,
Grasmere,
Cumbria.

27 June 1981

Dear Sir,

    I am writing to ask for advice on portable radios.

    I am looking for a model in the price range £70 – £100. My job involves a lot of travelling, so I particularly want a small light model with reasonable sound quality and reception. I wonder if you could recommend a suitable model.

              Yours faithfully,

              Joe Parks

b

Dear Sue,
    I've been having some trouble with Johnny recently, so I'd like to ask you for some advice.
    As you know, he's just started at the new school and he seemed to be enjoying it at first, but last week his teacher rang me to ask why he was absent. I got such a shock since I'd just sent him off to school. She said he'd been absent every day last week, and when he came home I found he'd been playing truant.
    He says he doesn't like the teacher and hasn't any friends. I'm really worried about him as he used to be such a cheerful, noisy little boy, and now he's silent and depressed.
    What do you think I should do?
              Love,
              Janet.

c

J. H. Harmer,
Market Consultancy Service,
Liverpool Street,
Slough.

15 May 1982

Rosalynn Beauty Products,
Milton Road,
Slough.

Dear Mr. Newton,

    Thank you for your letter of 29 March 1982, asking for advice on the marketability of your product. We have carried out a sales survey on your behalf, and in our opinion the product will sell well as there is nothing quite like it on the market.

    The demand for this type of cosmetic seems to be mainly among the 18 – 25 age group and we therefore suggest that advertising be aimed at this age range.

    A full report is enclosed.

              Yours faithfully,

              J. H. Harmer

d

Since you are obviously so unhappy and restricted at home, it seems to me that your best course would be to leave home and move into your own flat. However, as you seem rather shy and are worried about your lack of self confidence, accepting a job in a different town may not be the answer. It can be difficult to make friends and establish an identity in a new job in a strange town, so changing your job may be too big a step. I would suggest remaining in your present job, where you have friends and colleagues, but moving out to a flat of your own somewhere in the town. Although it may be difficult to break away, I am sure your relationship with your parents will improve once you have moved away and asserted your independence.

LANGUAGE SUMMARY   *1 Expressing advice and recommendation*
The following tables summarise expressions for asking for advice
and giving recommendations:
(i) Advice

I am writing to ask I would be grateful I wonder		if	you could help me (with . . .) you could advise me (on . . .) you could recommend . . .
I would	like appreciate be grateful for		some advice on . . . some help with . . .

(ii) Recommendation

I would	advise recommend suggest		. . . ing	
In my opinion you	should ought	to		. . .
I would advise you to				
It seems to me that your best course is to				

2 Linking words for reason-giving
Most letters of advice and recommendation state the writer's
reasons for seeking advice or making a particular suggestion. The
following tables summarise linking words for reason-giving:

In my opinion you should look for a new job	**because** **as** **since**	you seem so unhappy in your present one.

Since **As**	you seem so unhappy in your present job		I suggest you look for a new one.
	You seem unhappy in your present job	**so** **therefore**	

Exercise 1
Combining

(i) You are giving advice to a friend who is depressed about his job. Think of reasons for the advice below and then join reason and advice together with a linking word from language summary 2.
1   You should change your job altogether, and retrain.
2   You should talk to your boss about the situation.
3   You should look for a job with another firm.
4   You should try to get a job abroad.
5   You should give up work altogether!

(ii) The following phrases are from your friend's letter to a Careers Advisory Service asking for advice on a new career. Think of possible reasons for the preferences he expresses, and then join reason and preference together with a linking word from language summary 2.
1   I would like a job involving languages.
2   I would like a job involving as little paperwork as possible.
3   I would like a job within a thirty-mile radius of Reading.
4   I would prefer not to work irregular hours.
5   I would prefer a job that involved meeting and talking to people.

Exercise 2
Free writing

(i) Write an introductory sentence *asking for* advice for each of the following letters. Use expressions from language summary 1 (Advice).
1   To a consumer magazine about buying a camera.
2   To a problem page about your son's girlfriend.
3   To a slimming magazine.
4   To your bank manager about investing your money.
5   To a friend who is keen on gardening, about your garden.

(ii) Write an introductory sentence *giving* advice for each of the following letters. Use expressions from language summary 1 (Recommendation).
1   To someone who has just moved to your town and is lonely.
2   To someone who is trying to give up smoking.
3   To someone who is looking for a flat in your town.
4   To someone who wants to learn English.
5   To someone who has just bought a new car.

Reference exercise

Abstract nouns
Look at these sentences:

I am becoming worried by my son's boxed(behaviour) . He has been

boxed(rather rude and aggressive) lately.

My son has become boxed(rather rude and aggressive) lately. I am

becoming worried by his boxed(behaviour) .

You can use a general abstract noun to refer forwards or backwards.

Choose a general abstract noun from this list to fill in the blanks in the sentences below:

problem   situation   matter   circumstances   idea   difficulties

1 I am writing to you to ask for advice on a .... I am rather depressed at work and would like to change my job.
2 Recently my aunt died and left me some money. I would like to invest it and would appreciate your advice on this ....
3 John and I are considering taking up an offer of a job in Japan. I would like to know what you think of this ....
4 Taking into account the .... you describe, I would recommend looking for a new job as soon as possible.
5 I am writing to ask for your advice about some .... I am experiencing at work.
6 My neighbour has always been very noisy but recently the .... has started to get out of control.

PARAGRAPH OUTLINE   A   Letters asking for advice can be organised like this:

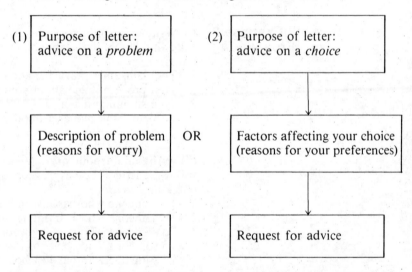

Look at the letters in the reading passage. How are they organised? Which is a letter about a *worry* and which is a letter about a *choice*?

B   Letters giving recommendations can be organised like this:

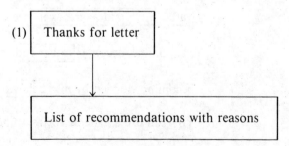

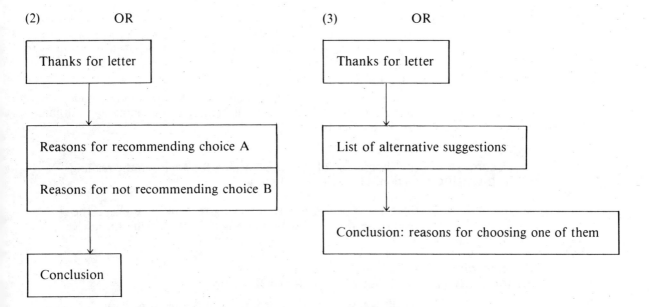

(2)   OR

```
┌─────────────────────┐
│ Thanks for letter   │
└─────────────────────┘
          │
          ▼
┌───────────────────────────────────────┐
│ Reasons for recommending choice A      │
├───────────────────────────────────────┤
│ Reasons for not recommending choice B  │
└───────────────────────────────────────┘
          │
          ▼
┌─────────────────────┐
│ Conclusion          │
└─────────────────────┘
```

(3)   OR

```
┌─────────────────────┐
│ Thanks for letter   │
└─────────────────────┘
          │
          ▼
┌───────────────────────────────────────┐
│ List of alternative suggestions        │
└───────────────────────────────────────┘
          │
          ▼
┌────────────────────────────────────────────┐
│ Conclusion: reasons for choosing one of them│
└────────────────────────────────────────────┘
```

Exercise 3 (i) This letter asking for advice is in muddled order. Rewrite it in a
Reordering more coherent order. Use paragraph outline A2.

Dear Aunt Joan,

I will be leaving school in July and hope to study English at college

and therefore would also be interested in applying for clerical work

because I feel this is the best way of getting to know the country

I am writing to ask for some advice on getting a job in England

I would be very grateful if you could give me any help or suggestions

as I know you have lived there for several years and have friends and contacts there,

so I would like to spend a year in England to improve my English

I would like to live with a family

I like children and have experience working with them

As well as this I have some office experience

so I would be interested in a job as an au pair or mother's help

51

Guided writing	(ii) Imagine that you are the mother or father of a teenage boy. Your son was recently caught shoplifting. It was a great shock to you, as he has always been so quiet and well behaved. He refuses to talk to you about it. Write a letter to a problem page using paragraph outline A1.

When you have finished, exchange letters with another student. Write a reply to his/her letter using any of the paragraph outlines for recommendations.

Exercise 4 Free writing	(i) Choose one of the letters asking for advice in the reading section, and write a reply to it.

(ii) Choose one of the letters giving recommendations in the reading section, and write the original letter asking for advice.

Exercise 5 Writing activity	Do this activity in groups of four. Work in two pairs: A and B, C and D.

Student A should turn to page 126 and look at activity C.
Student B should turn to page 128 and look at activity I.

Student C should turn to page 128 and look at activity G.
Student D should turn to page 132 and look at activity Q.

When you have written your letters, exchange them with the other pair. Read the letters and write a reply.

Unit 8 Postcards

Describing static and moving features

Focus in a description

Reading   Read these holiday postcards. Then match the front with the back of the cards.

a

1

Dear Joan,

The cottage is delightful – it's in a small village in the middle of rich rolling countryside. There's an apple orchard at the back, & a small garden at the front which runs down to a small stream + a wooden bridge. All around, there are gentle hills + cornfields & meadows. A line of trees along the hilltop, & woods to the right. It really is beautiful and peaceful!

See you soon,
David

b

Dear Mary   **2**

From my window I can see gently sloping green pastures with cows grazing – the bells clang all day and night, it's very relaxing to listen to. Down in the valley is the main part of the village – I can just see the church spire. Beyond that, the snow capped mountains. You can see really steep black rocks and a waterfall, and the snow line is high above us – we watch it change colour through the day, from white to pink to a deep red at sunset – it's absolutely idyllic!

From
Wendy

c

3

Dear Brian,

Well, we've been here five days now, and have all kinds of weather. It's a very dramatic coastline, with steeply plunging dark cliffs, and beautiful white sandy coves which are completely deserted – the water's terribly cold though! The cliffs stretch away for miles to the west; in the distance are a group of small deserted islands. The nearest village is five miles away along a bumpy road. There was a terrific storm two days ago, huge white waves crashing against the cliffs, and our windows were covered in spray – I wouldn't like to live here in the winter!   Sue and Peter

Dear Stephen,   **4**

The landscape is very barren and lonely and the soil is very poor, just heather and peat and a few brown-looking lakes. But no trees at all! You can walk for miles and miles, and not see a soul! Behind our hotel there is a place which the locals say is haunted by ghosts – a pile of huge cracked rocks which look as though they have just been abandoned by some being from outer space... I wouldn't like to go there alone, especially at night! We're looking forward to seeing you.

Bye for now,
Sally and Andrew

d

LANGUAGE SUMMARY When you are describing scenery, you have to show the relation of one place or feature to another. Features in landscape can be seen as *static* ('to the right of the house is a small wood') or *moving*, leading somewhere ('the road winds past the house'). A lively and interesting description will contain both *static* and *moving* features. When describing place relations you can say what is *all around*, what is *near*, what is *far away*, what is *on each side* of you, and what is *above and below* a certain point.

The following table gives some linking words for place relations:

1 Linking words for place relations
(i) Static

Surroundings	The house	is set among is surrounded	by	rolling hills.
	All around As far as the eye can see		(there) are	
Near + Far	In the	foreground background distance	(there) is	a church.
	A	little long	way off	
On each side	To the	left right	of	
	Near Next to In front of To the rear of Beyond		the house	
Up + Down	On the hillside On the brow of the hill In the valley			there is a tree.
	At the	top bottom	of the cliff	
	Below Above	the house		

(ii) Moving

Fields Woods	stretch as far as	the | horizon. | water's edge.
A road A path	skirts leads to/into	| village. a | wood.
	crosses	| plain a | field | river
	curves | past winds |	a | town. | building.
Mountains Hills	slope down to rise up from	the | village. | plain.
The river stream	flows | into runs |	a lake.
	winds | past flows |	the house.

Exercise 1
Completion

Do this activity in pairs.
Look at the picture and discuss it with your partner.
Then fill in the blanks in the description below.

The house is .... hills and fields. .... is a little stream
which winds .... and .... is a small wood. There is a
.... path which .... from .... into ....
.... is a small neatly-kept garden and .... is a
cherry orchard .... are cornfields and .... is a low
ridge of hills. .... you can see a line of trees.

Exercise 2
Rewriting

Make the description below more lively by including verbs of movement.

There is a road in front of my window. There are fields all around. To the left is a clump of trees. There is a river. In the middle distance there is a bridge. Beyond that there is a farmhouse and some cottages. In the far distance you can see the sea.

PARAGRAPH OUTLINE

When you are describing a scene or a landscape, you can make it easier for your reader to visualise it by:

or by

A   describing features from near to far, like this:

B   giving your description a focus and describing outwards from a central point, like this:

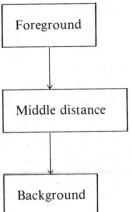

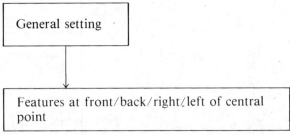

(as in a description of where a house or village is situated)

(as in a view from a window)

Exercise 3
Reordering

(i) This description of a view is in muddled order. Reorder it to make it easier to visualise. Use paragraph outline A.

In the far distance you can see the mountains outlined against the sky.
A path winds through the meadow, and down through pinewoods to the village.
Beyond the village are flat, open fields with a river flowing through them.
Directly in front of the window is a sloping meadow covered in primroses, with a few wooden chalets to the right and a stone barn to the left.
I can see a beautiful mountain landscape from my window.
I can see a cluster of red roofs and a grey church spire in the valley.
Beyond the fields, the ground rises again to a line of low hills, their slopes thickly covered with pine trees.

Guided writing   (ii) Read these notes and draw a rough sketch of the scene. Then write a description of the scene using paragraph outline B.

General surroundings	farm house in open country and pasture
To the right of the farm	road curves round leads to village
To the left of the farm	cow sheds farmyard haybarn
To the back	ground rises steeply small hill clump of trees
At the front	fields run down to the river
Beyond the river	water meadows and then cornfields

Exercise 4   Choose either (i) or (ii).
Free writing   (i) Write a description of one of these pictures and when you have finished, exchange descriptions with another student. Can he/she tell which picture you were describing?

(ii) Imagine your dream house in the country.
What would it be like?
Where would it be?
What would the surroundings be like?
Write a description of the house and its setting *or*
                        the view from one of the upstairs windows.

Exercise 5   Choose either (i) or (ii).
Writing activity   (i) Do this activity in pairs.
Together, choose one of the following words:
a   dramatic
b   peaceful
c   lonely
d   majestic

Close your eyes for two minutes and imagine a scene that suggests one of the above adjectives.
Then open your eyes and describe the scene to your partner.
Compare impressions and then write a description of the scene you imagined.

(ii) At home, find an old holiday photo, or postcard of a country scene.
Write a description of the view pictured on the photo or card and exchange your description with another student.
Can you draw his description?

Unit 9 'Which' reports

Organising a factual report

Comparison and contrast

Reading   Read the text on portable radios and use the information in it to complete this table.

Name of model	Country of origin	Price	Size	Weight	Reception	Sound quality
			L		xxxx	xxxx
			M			
					x	xx
	Taiwan		S			

xxxx = best

x   = worst

Portable Radios

Four portable radios from different countries were compared with respect to price, size, weight, reception of broadcasts and sound quality.

The 'Harmony' from Japan was, at £260, the most expensive. It was also the largest and the heaviest model, but we found that it had the best reception and sound quality.

The Austrian 'Playboy' model was smaller and lighter than the 'Harmony' model, weighing 5 kg whereas the 'Harmony' weighed 7 kg. It was similar to the 'Harmony' as regards sound quality, but the reception was not quite as good.

The 'Crystal' from Hong Kong was similar to the 'Playboy' in size and weight, but differed in sound quality and reception which were much poorer. However, it only cost £75 while the 'Playboy' cost £100.

The 'Tango' from Taiwan was the cheapest of the four radios. It was also the smallest and the lightest, weighing 2 kg less than the 'Crystal' or the 'Playboy'. As far as sound quality and reception were concerned, it performed better than the 'Crystal' but not as well as the 'Playboy' or the 'Harmony'.

LANGUAGE SUMMARY The following tables summarise ways of *expressing similarities and differences* and *linking words for comparison and contrast.*

1 Expressing similarities and differences

A and B	were compared with respect to weight.
A resembles B A and B are similar A is similar to B	in that they both weigh 5 kg.
A differs from B A and B differ A is different from B	in weight. as regards weight. with regard to weight. with respect to weight. as far as weight is concerned.
B is not as heavy as A.	
A is heavier than B.	

2 Linking words for comparison and contrast
If you want to compare the relative size, weight, price, etc of two things, you can use **whereas, while** or **in contrast**.

A weighs 3 kg	**whereas** **while** **. In contrast**	B weighs 4 kg.

If you want to contrast the advantages and disadvantages of two things, you can use **however, but** or **although**.

	A was more expensive Car A was more economical	**. However** **but**	it was better quality than B. car B was faster and more comfortable.	
Although	car A was more economical, A was more expensive,			
	A was more expensive. It was,	**however,**		better quality than B.
	Car A was more economical. Car B was,			faster and more comfortable.

59

Both/neither/all/none

Look at these sentences:

We examined two radios. The two radios cost around £50. The two radios did not have good sound quality.

We examined ┌two radios┐. ┌Both┐ cost around £50. ┌Neither┐ had good sound quality.

We tested four televisions. The televisions cost around £300. The televisions did not have particularly good colour.

We tested ┌four televisions┐. ┌All┐ cost around £300. ┌None┐ had particularly good colour.

You can refer back and avoid repetition by using **both, neither, all** or **none**.

Use **both, neither, all** or **none** to avoid repetition in these sentences:
1 We received details of two new brands of shampoo this week. The two brands are not on the market yet.
2 We did trials on six small cars. The six cars did not cost more than £3000.
3 I went to four restaurants. The four restaurants had a lively atmosphere and good cooking.
4 Our representative went to two hotels in Zermatt. The two hotels offered first-class accommodation and good service.
5 We looked at two houses. The two houses were modern and spacious but did not have gardens.

Exercise 1
Completion

Here is a table comparing the advantages and disadvantages of two small cars. Use the information in the table and the language in the language summary to help you complete the passage on the opposite page comparing the two cars.

	FIAT 126	RENAULT 4
Price	£3100	£3800
Economy	46 mpg	40 mpg
Convenience	rather cramped seats tiny boot	very comfortable seats large luggage space
Performance	cruising speed 50 mph poor acceleration slowed down by hills	cruising speed 50 mph poor acceleration underpowered on hills

This week we took a look at two small, about-town cars and compared them .... price, economy, convenience and performance.

The two models .... considerably in price, the Fiat costing £3100, ... the Renault cost .... The Fiat was also .... than the Renault, its average fuel consumption being 46 mpg .... that of the Renault was .... The Renault 4 was, however, ... than the Fiat, with more comfortable seating and a .... luggage space. The two cars were .... performance; both had a cruising speed of around ...., both had .... and both were ....

Exercise 2
Guided writing

Look at the following table comparing two other small cars. Use the data to write sentences comparing them.

Use language from the language summary and write about ten sentences. (The sentences need not be connected to form a paragraph.)

eg The Mini was more economical than the Simca.

The Mini was more economical but the Simca was roomier.

	Mini 1000	**Simca 1000**
Price	£3000	£3200
Economy	45 mpg	45 mpg
Comfort	not much legroom very small boot	roomy seating big boot
Performance	top speed 70 mph good roadholding easy to handle	top speed 70 mph good roadholding easy to handle

PARAGRAPH OUTLINE In the reading passage at the start of this unit, the writer describes each radio in turn, like this:

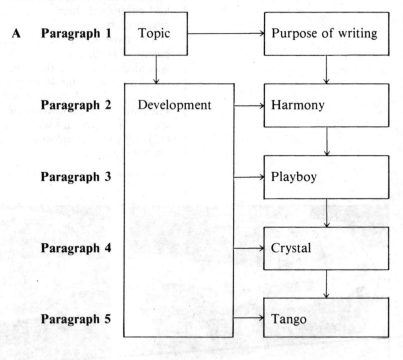

In the passage in Exercise 1, the information is organised under headings, like this:

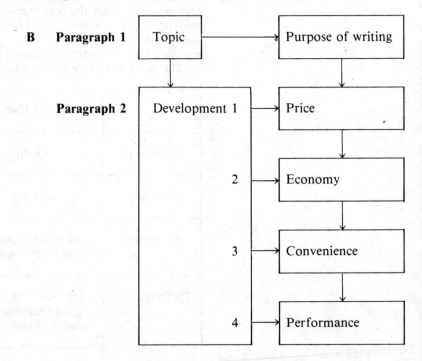

Exercise 3
Rewriting

(i) Now rewrite the reading passage. Reorganise the information under headings, like this:

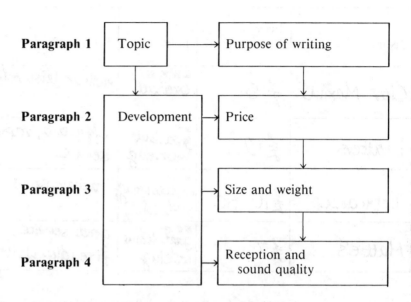

Guided writing

(ii) Use the information below to write a passage comparing two family saloon cars, the Cavalier and the Peugeot, following paragraph outline B.

There was plenty of legroom in the back of the Peugeot.

Both cars had plenty of room in the boot.

The Peugeot had a good heating system and the fresh air vents worked well.

The Cavalier's average fuel consumption was 26 mpg.

The seating in the back of the Cavalier was cramped.

The Cavalier cost £4242.

The heating and ventilation in the Cavalier was not as good.

The Cavalier's performance was rapid and smooth: the car cruised comfortably at 70 mph.

The Peugeot cost £4365.

The Peugeot was slower and the acceleration was not so lively.

The Peugeot's average fuel consumption was 31 mpg.

(iii) You are a journalist and have been asked to write a report on restaurants for a consumer magazine. You investigated four restaurants and made notes on your findings. Use the data to write a short report, following paragraph outline A.

Name	Price of 3-course meal	Food	Service	Atmosphere + Decor
Chez Maxim	£15	**** excellent	rather leisurely	elegant, luxurious
Platters	£12	** good, but unexciting	efficient, rapid service	crowded, noisy
Tropicana	£10.50	* disappointing, food cold	rather slow	dull
Mattie's	£7	*** good home cooking	good service, friendly waiter	lively, cheerful atmosphere

Exercise 4
Free writing

Read the following dialogue between a customer and a travel agent and use the information in it to complete the table:

Travel agent Good morning, madam. What can I do for you?

Mrs Brown Good morning. I'd like some information on organised holidays, please. My husband and I and our two children want to spend a fortnight in Britain in June.

Travel agent What sort of holiday did you have in mind? Do you want to stay in one place or travel around?

Mrs Brown Well, that really depends on price.

Travel agent The cheapest thing you could do, of course, is to rent a cottage somewhere and do your own catering. For example, this firm, Summerhouse, specialises in rented cottages in the West Country — prices for a cottage start at around £70 a week.

Mrs Brown I see, but that might be a bit restricting.

Travel agent Of course, you could always stay in a hotel — that would be more comfortable. Holilux offer a fortnight in a luxury hotel, for example, at around £60 per person per week.

Mrs Brown Is there any way of combining car rental with a hotel holiday? We'd like to see a bit more of the country.

Travel agent Yes, this firm, Wheelers, specialise in the planned itinerary. You pick the car up from London or Edinburgh, and drive off for two weeks, staying at up to five hotels from this list.

Mrs Brown	Is that very expensive?
Travel agent	Not really; in fact it works out at about £680 for a family of four for two weeks.
Mrs Brown	I see. How about camping holidays? Do you do those?
Travel agent	Yes. In fact by far the most flexible arrangement is this one by Eurocanvas. You can stay at up to ten different campsites in the British Isles — and with car hire this works out at about £80 per person for the two weeks. Of course, it is less comfortable than a hotel or cottage holiday, but all the campsites are fully equipped to a very high standard, and there are first-class facilities for all ages.
Mrs Brown	Yes, that sounds ideal. I'd like to make a booking now if I may....

Name of holiday firm	Price for 4 people for 2 weeks	Type of accommodation	Comfort and convenience	Variety and flexibility

Now write a report for a consumer magazine, comparing the different holidays with respect to price, accommodation offered, comfort and variety. Arrange your report as in either of the paragraph outlines on page 64.

Exercise 5
Writing activity

Do this activity in groups of four.
Find one item that you all own (eg camera, record player, radio ...) and then decide on aspects for comparison (price, reliability, durability, etc).
Compare the items. Say which aspects you are pleased with and which you are dissatisfied with. When you have finished, write a report.

Unit 10 Sci Fi

Combining narrative and description

Reading (i) Spacecraft Z101 is on a mission to the planet Zelda. Here is an account of the discovery of Zelda that Captain Qualcast, of Z101, transmitted back to Earth on Day 152 of the mission. Because of the time-warp between Zelda and Earth, the account arrived in muddled order. Can you arrange the events in the order in which they occurred?

We then deployed four ground transport vehicles which went out in different directions to explore. They were going to make observations about the terrain.

We tape-recorded the insects' music and played it back over the spacecraft's loudspeaker. Each time we played different sounds the insects regrouped in a new formation. So we assume that the sounds are part of a communication system but we cannot discover its meaning.

At 500 kilometres above the surface of Planet Zelda, we went into orbit, and made ten orbits around the planet to observe its surface and atmosphere.

While the ground transport vehicles were away from the spacecraft, the sky darkened and we saw that we were surrounded by a cloud of flying insects.

The insects are now hovering around the spacecraft without moving closer or interfering with us. This suggests that they are observing us, in the same way as we are observing them.

After we had completed ten orbits, we landed on the central land mass, and immediately took photographs of the sky and land, and collected samples of the soils and vegetation.

They filled the air around the craft, but did not attack. We attempted to capture some in nets, but they flew out of reach every time.

(ii) Opposite are some observations made by Qualcast, and some of the photographs he took. Draw a line to connect each observation with the photograph it describes.

a The planet is 25,000 k in diameter, and its surface is divided into seas and land masses. Its general appearance is similar to that of Earth.

b The atmosphere is humid and cloudy, but non-toxic. The sky is light pink, with two suns.

c The ground is slightly hilly, and covered with dense and luxuriant vegetation of a bright green colour, which extends as far as the eye can see.

d The insects are about 15 cm long with a wing span of 30 cm. They have a long, narrow body, and four oval wings which are blue-green in colour.

e The most striking thing about them was the sound they produced. By moving their wings, they made a tune of three or four notes.

f The soil is a soft yellow mud and must be very fertile, for it is covered in shrubs and small plants with red heart-shaped flowers.

LANGUAGE SUMMARY Most stories are not just a list of events, but combine *narrative* and *description*. Sometimes your story will *move forward* as you narrate events, and sometimes it will *stand still* as you look around you.

You have already practised narrative and description as separate skills. This unit will practise *combining* narrative and description.

Exercise 1
Combining

Do this activity in pairs.
Reread the reading passages (i) and (ii) and then discuss how you could combine Qualcast's narrative of events with the descriptions of the things he saw.

Where would you insert the descriptions in the narrative?

Exercise 2
Completion

Complete Qualcast's diary of Day 153 of the mission. Insert descriptions of the things that Qualcast saw.

DAY 153

Today we circled Zelda and landed on the far side of the planet — the side that is not visible from Earth. I peered out of the window and saw a strange landscape. . . . .
. . . .
. . . .
. . . .

Sam and I decided to make a short reconnaissance trip, so we took out one of the ground transport vehicles and drove about two . . . . kilometres through . . . .
. . . .
. . . .

All around us were . . . .
. . . .

Then suddenly, we saw a strange object in front of us . . . .

It appeared to be some sort of building. We were curious, but . . . . rather wary, so we circled the object carefully, and looked at it . . . . . . from all sides . . . .
. . . .

There was a strange humming sound coming from the object. We . . . . photographed it, and started back towards Z101. We had gone . . . . . . about 200 metres when I looked over my shoulder and suddenly . . . . . saw . . . .
. . . .
. . . .

Exercise 3
Guided writing

When you are writing a story, you want to keep the reader's interest, so it is important to maintain a balance between narrative and description.

If your descriptions are too long, the story will become static. Your reader will become bored and will want to move forward. If your story does not contain enough description, it will read like a catalogue of events. Your reader will be tired and will need time to stand still.

The following activity will practise telling a story to an audience.
Do this activity in pairs.
Work out a ghost story together, but do not write it down yet.
Use the following questions to guide you:

When did it happen?
Where were you staying?
What was the house like?
What was the surrounding countryside like?
When did you first notice something was wrong?
What was the first thing that happened?
What did you hear?
What did you see?

What did you feel?
What did you do?
What happened next?
What did you hear?
    see?
    feel?
What did you do in the end?

When you have finished, join up with another pair.
Tell them your story. Try to create an atmosphere! Now listen to theirs and ask questions if anything is unclear. Then write down your story. (You can use the best ideas from both stories if you like.)

Exercise 4
Free writing

Write your own science fiction story. It should include descriptions of the following things:

and you should narrate the following incidents:

a dust storm
falling in a river
an eclipse of the sun
a chase.

Exercise 5
Writing activity

Do this activity in groups of four.
Decide together on a *type* of story (adventure/romantic/sci-fi, etc.).
Each person should then write a short description of the following:

Student 1 a house
   2 a landscape
   3 a person
   4 an object

Read your descriptions out to each other.
Now each write a story, including all four descriptions in your narrative.
Read out your stories to each other when you have finished.

Unit 11 Beginnings and endings in a story

Reading   Here are six different ways a story could start:

> 'That's it!' thought Jim. 'Of course that's what I'll do.'
> The idea came to him as he was walking down the road.
>
> > Once there was a man whose name was Jim.
> > His wife was called Kate, and they had three
> > children.
>
> Jim often had strange ideas
> but this was the strangest.
>
> > There was a man called Jim who lived
> > in Birmingham. One day as he was
> > walking to work he had a good idea.
>
> Jim was 1.70m tall with blue eyes and fair hair. He
> lived in a small house in Birmingham.
>
> The first thing you noticed about Jim was his eyes.

Which openings most make you want to read the story? Which
openings least encourage you to read on?

LANGUAGE SUMMARY   Here are some suggestions for *starting* stories:

DON'T EXPLAIN — MYSTIFY!

(i)	*Make the reader want to know more about what is going to happen in your story*	The strange thing was, he said, how they screamed every night at midnight.
(ii)	*Make the reader want to know more about the character in your story*	'If I'm out of my mind, it's all right with me,' thought Moses Herzog.
(iii)	*Make a generalisation. The reader will want to know how you support it*	All happy families are alike but an unhappy family is unhappy after its own fashion.
(iv)	*Start with a conversation*	'Gracie darling, will you marry me?' 'Yes.' '*What?*' 'Yes.'

(v)	*Start with a short sentence*	I am an invisible man.
(vi)	*Talk as if you and your reader had shared the same experiences*	You know how it is there early in the morning in Havana . . .

Exercise 1
Rewriting

Suggest new openings to replace these:

> One Sunday afternoon John and Anne decided to go for a walk.

(a story about a strange discovery . . .)

> Angela Harris lived in Manchester. Her husband was called John, and they had two small children called Mary and Susan.

(a story about a love-affair . . .)

> Appleton is a small village in the south of England. It has a church, two shops and a pub . . .

(a story about a village quarrel)

Exercise 2
Free writing

Here are the dust-jackets from some books.
Write what you imagine might be the opening paragraph of each book.

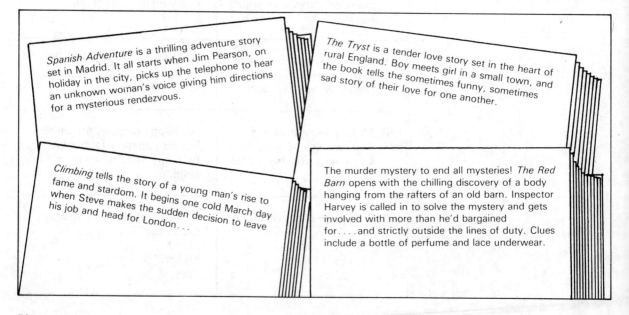

Spanish Adventure is a thrilling adventure story set in Madrid. It all starts when Jim Pearson, on holiday in the city, picks up the telephone to hear an unknown woman's voice giving him directions for a mysterious rendezvous.

The Tryst is a tender love story set in the heart of rural England. Boy meets girl in a small town, and the book tells the sometimes funny, sometimes sad story of their love for one another.

Climbing tells the story of a young man's rise to fame and stardom. It begins one cold March day when Steve makes the sudden decision to leave his job and head for London. . .

The murder mystery to end all mysteries! The Red Barn opens with the chilling discovery of a body hanging from the rafters of an old barn. Inspector Harvey is called in to solve the mystery and gets involved with more than he'd bargained for. . . .and strictly outside the lines of duty. Clues include a bottle of perfume and lace underwear.

Exercise 3
Free writing

Below is a summary of each chapter in a novel called *No Escape*.
Write the opening paragraph for any one of the chapters.
When you have finished, pass it to another student who will try to guess which chapter the paragraph opens.

Energetic young man tired of his job.
Changes job and town.
Meets very strange woman.
She falls in love with him.
He falls in love with his new boss who is married.
Travel abroad.
Death of the strange woman.
Hero and mistress suspected.
Escape to another country.
Tension when husband finds out.
Happy ending; for the hero only.

LANGUAGE SUMMARY

A story can *end* in different ways:

(i) *Many stories end with a conclusion*	. . . and they all lived happily ever after.
(ii) *But you don't have to end with a conclusion. You can end with a question*	'In Heaven's name, where is Beth?'
(iii) *You can end in suspense . . .*	But they never did find out who had stolen the teacups . . .
(iv) *Or you can end with a surprise!*	. . . Lady Anne made no sign of interfering. She had been dead for two hours.

Exercise 4
Free writing

Go back to the short stories you started in Exercise 1.
Choose one and complete it, giving it an interesting or unexpected ending.

Exercise 5
Writing activity

Write the beginning of a short story (about half a page), and then exchange stories with another student.
Write the endings for each other's stories.

Unit 12 Murder in the study

Organising an argument: drawing conclusions and giving evidence

Reading   This is a plan of the country house of Major and Lady McTavish:

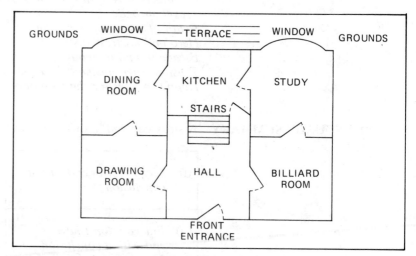

This is the story of the murder:

At 10 pm, Lucy the maid went into the study to close the windows and found the Reverend Makepeace dead on the floor. He had been stabbed with a kitchen knife. Lucy recognised the knife, and said it had been lying on the kitchen table earlier that evening.

The police were very puzzled by the case. The only doors to the study are from the kitchen and the billiard room, and these rooms were full of people all the time that the Reverend Makepeace was in the study. The people in the billiard room and the kitchen saw no one go in or out of the rooms during this time.

Colonel Smythe, Major McTavish, and the Reverend were playing billiards in the billiard room. The first game ended at about 8.45, and the Reverend Makepeace excused himself from the second game, saying he had to finish off a sermon for the next day. He went into the study.

Lucy the maid and Parkin the butler were in the kitchen from 8 pm to 10 pm. At 8.30 Lucy took coffee to the ladies in the drawing room, and Parkin took port to the gentlemen in the billiard room. They returned to the kitchen about five minutes later.

Lady McTavish and Dame Maverick were talking in the drawing room from 8 pm to 10 pm. Mrs Hodge and Pamela stayed in the dining room to watch television. Mrs Hodge went through to the drawing room to join the others for coffee at 8.30 but Pamela said she would stay to see the end of the programme. Angela Dumondo-Balcombe was walking alone in the grounds. She came in at 8.45. She changed her muddy shoes in the hall, poured herself a cup of coffee in the drawing room, and went on into the dining room where Pamela was still watching television.

An assumption made on the basis of partial evidence is called a *hypothesis*. For each of the six hypotheses below, circle the appropriate letter according to whether the hypothesis is true or false.

If you circle all the letters correctly you will find an important clue.

	True	False
(i) Colonel Symthe could not have done it, because Major McTavish would have seen him leave the billiard room.	W	B
(ii) Lucy could have killed the Reverend Makepeace in the study at 8.30 pm.	A	I
(iii) Lady McTavish could not have left the drawing room between 8.30 pm and 9 pm.	N	L
(iv) Mrs Hodge could have gone to the study on her way to the drawing room.	C	D
(v) Angela could have entered the study at any time while she was alone outside.	O	O
(vi) Parkin could have waited for the Reverend Makepeace in the study after he had served port in the billiard room.	N	W

LANGUAGE SUMMARY

A hypothesis is a *provisional explanation based on partial evidence*. Because a hypothesis is only a *temporary* explanation, we cannot always be certain that it is correct.

Sometimes we will be absolutely sure that the hypothesis is correct (there is plenty of evidence, and nothing seems to contradict it). Sometimes we will be less certain about our hypothesis (there is not enough evidence and a few puzzling facts). When you write hypotheses, therefore, you will have to do two things: (i) say *how likely* your hypothesis is, and (ii) produce *evidence to support* your hypothesis.

The following tables summarise some ways of *expressing likelihood* (or unlikelihood!) and some ways of *linking hypothesis and evidence*.

1 Expressing degrees of likelihood
You can express likelihood by using a phrase like 'it is possible' or a verb like 'must' or 'may'. The expressions in the first table are more *formal* than those in the second table overleaf.

most likely ↓ *least likely*	It is	certain probable likely possible	that	the murderer is/is not a young man.
				the man committed the crime. the man did not commit the crime.

most likely	The murderer	must/cannot could/could not	be a young woman.
↓ least likely	Pamela	may/may not might/might not	have a brown hair. have committed the crime.

2 Linking words for hypothesis and evidence
The evidence can come before the hypothesis, like this:

Evidence		Hypothesis
The study window was open	so therefore	someone could have entered the study from outside.

Or the hypothesis can come before the evidence, like this:

Hypothesis		Evidence
Someone could have entered the study from outside	because since as	the study window was open.

Exercise 1
Combining

Match suspect and hypothesis in the following exercise.
Use an expression from the language summary to connect the two.

Major McTavish Lucy Parkin	. . . . . been in the drawing room when the crime was committed.
Dame Maverick	. . . . . entered the study between 8 pm and 8.45 pm.
Mrs Hodge	. . . . . left the billiard room.
Angela .	. . . . . left the kitchen between 8.35 pm and 10 pm.

Find evidence in the text to support the hypotheses and then connect evidence and hypothesis using language from the language summary.

**Exercise 2
Completion**

(i) Here is a conversation between Detective Inspector Harvey and Sergeant Holmes, his assistant.
Fill in the blanks.
The first letters of blanks 1, 5, 6, 8, 13 and 16 (but not in that order) will give you the name of the murderer.

Harvey ....1 could have done it. She could have climbed in through the ....2 ....3 and stabbed Makepeace as he sat at the desk.

Holmes No, how could she have taken the ....4?

Harvey Well, she could have gone into the kitchen while ....5 and ....6 were out, and taken the knife, and then waited in the ....7 till ....8 came in.

Holmes No, she wouldn't have had time to get back to the ....9 ....10. She was coming into the house at the same ....11 as Makepeace was going into the study. And besides her shoes were ....12. If she had ....13 the study she would have left ....14 on the floor, and there were no traces of ....15.

Harvey Yes, you're right, ...16 couldn't have done it. But who could it have been?

Holmes Ah, I think I've got it, Sir!

(ii) Use the language in the language summaries to fill in the blanks in this police report.

WEST WILLOW CONSTABULARY   *Ref. No. 624/5AC*

One possibility is that Angela committed the crime.

The study was empty until 8.45 .... she .... climbed through the window before Makepeace came in. Lucy and Parkin were out of the kitchen between 8.30 and 8.35. .... she .... entered the kitchen and taken the knife then. The study was still empty .... she .... hidden there until 8.45 when Makepeace came in.

However, she .... had time to do this, ... she was seen returning to the front door at 8.45. Moreover, the ground outside was very muddy, ... if she had entered the study she .... left traces of mud on the floor.

.... Angela .... committed the crime.

77

PARAGRAPH OUTLINE   The information in the police report is organised like this:

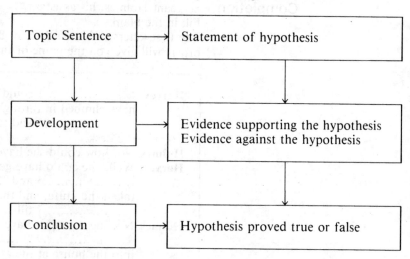

Topic Sentence	→	Statement of hypothesis
Development	→	Evidence supporting the hypothesis / Evidence against the hypothesis
Conclusion	→	Hypothesis proved true or false

Exercise 3
Guided writing

Use the organisation given in the paragraph outline to write a similar report on Pamela.

The following notes from Detective Inspector Harvey's notebook will help you:

TIME	EVIDENCE	HYPOTHESIS
8.30	Mrs Hodge left the dining room and Pamela was alone.	– could have opened the dining room window.
8.30 – 8.35	Lucy and Parkin were out of the kitchen.	– could have gone through the kitchen into study, taking the knife from the table.
8.35 – 8.45	There was no one in the study.	– could have hidden in the study.
8.45	Makepeace came into the study and sat at his desk.	– could have stabbed him in the back.
8.45 – 8.50 ?	Angela came in, but spent some time changing her shoes and getting a cup of coffee before she went into the dining room.	. . . . ?

Exercise 4
Free writing

Unfortunately, while Harvey and Holmes were discussing the case, Pamela slipped out of the house and got away. Here are some of the clues the police found:

(i)   Her wardrobe was bare, and a small suitcase was gone.
(ii) No one saw her leave the house, but the drawing room window was open, and there were footprints in the flower bed.
(iii) Her bicycle was found at the station.
(iv) A train left the station for Dover at 11 pm.
(v)   Boats leave Dover for France and Belgium.

Write a police report summarising the evidence and making hypotheses about Pamela's departure.

Exercise 5
Writing activity

Invent five or six more clues to help the police solve the mystery of Pamela's disappearance and write them down.

When you have finished, exchange your list of clues with someone else and write a hypothesis based on their evidence.

Check with them to see if your hypotheses match their original intentions.

Unit 13 Speeches

Organising argument: headings

Reading

> Ladies and Gentlemen, I am here tonight to put forward the proposals for the new Town Hall. This will be located in George Street, and will replace the existing building in Church Street.
>
> A new town hall has been necessary for some time. The present building is old-fashioned, cramped and inconvenient. It is impossible to work efficiently in these surroundings.
>
> As for the suggestion that the project is a waste of public money, — the building in fact represents a valuable investment of public funds. The construction of the building will provide employment for many people, and the building itself will incorporate public facilities such as a library and an art gallery.
>
> To sum up, the project will be of great value, not only to those directly concerned, but also to the public as a whole.

> I would like to oppose the building of the new town hall on a number of counts.
>
> The building would be a disgraceful waste of public money, which could far more usefully be spent on the social services or education. Moreover, the site in George Street has been reserved for some time for a public park and the construction of the new town hall would mean abandoning this plan. The new building, incidentally, will be something of an eyesore, and will not harmonise in any way with its surroundings.
>
> To turn to the question of employment, workers will only be needed on the project for a year or two and will have to find new jobs elsewhere after that. The project will not be of any lasting benefit.
>
> In conclusion, I would like to say that I consider this project a shocking waste of money at a time of financial hardship.

Here is the report of the first speech as it appeared in the *Torbury Herald* the next day. The journalist who wrote it was rather tired and dozed off during the speech so the report is rather confused and inaccurate. Read the report and correct any mistakes.

At a meeting in Torbury Community Centre last night, Councillor Harper put forward proposals for the new library. He confirmed that this would be situated in Church Street, replacing the existing building in George Street.

He stated that a new hall was necessary because the old one was in a state of disrepair. Turning to the question of cost, he denied that the project was wasteful and suggested that large numbers of people would be employed in the new library. He added that the building would contain a museum and an art gallery and concluded that the project would be of great benefit to those interested in culture in Torbury.

LANGUAGE SUMMARY

1   Note taking

When you are making notes for a speech or taking notes from somebody else's speech, you will need to list the main points of the argument under headings.

When you are writing notes you can leave out all the words that are not essential to the sense. These words are usually:

articles
auxiliary verbs
personal pronouns
relative pronouns
impersonal subjects
prepositions if not essential to meaning.

But you must always make sure that the meaning is clear.

When you are giving a speech or reporting someone else's arguments, you may need to use certain words and expressions to make it clear when you are making a new point. If you are taking notes from a speech these words will help you to realise when the speaker is moving on to a different point and when you need a new heading. The following table summarises some linking words for argument.

2   Linking words for argument
(i) Starting off

Firstly, To begin with, As a start,	I think I feel I would like to say	that ...
The first point I would like to make is		

(ii) Changing the subject

As for Turning to To turn to	X
	the question of X
As far as	X is concerned

(iii) Concluding

In all, In short, In brief, On the whole, In conclusion, To sum up,	I feel that ... I think that ... it is clear that ... the proposals are ...

3 Reporting speech

The most common way of reporting a speech is, of course, 'he said that'. However, you can also *tell, suggest, promise, deny, ask,* etc. And these verbs should be used to give variety in a long piece of represented speech.

SAYING	He	said stated	that
TELLING		told me explained described	that that/how how
ASKING		asked enquired	if whether
SUGGESTING		proposed suggested put forward the idea	that
STATING AN OPINION OR POINT OF VIEW		asserted argued claimed pointed out	
SAYING A REPORT IS NOT TRUE		denied confirmed admitted	
MAKING A FURTHER POINT		added continued went on to say	
PROMISING		promised	
WARNING		threatened warned	
IMPLYING		implied suggested	
REVEALING NEW INFORMATION		disclosed revealed	
CONCLUDING		concluded summed up by saying	

Exercise 1
Note-taking

(i) Make notes on the first speech under the headings given below.

(ii) Make notes on the second speech. Organise your notes under headings.

Councillor Harper
(For)
1) need for new building

2) cost

3) facilities

4) conclusion

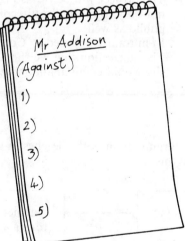

Mr Addison
(Against)
1)

2)

3)

4)

5)

Exercise 2
Completion

Fill in the blanks in this report of the second speech in the reading passage.

Mr Addison opposed the proposals for a number of reasons. He claimed that ...., arguing that. .... He pointed out that .... He added that .... and that .... On the question of employment, he asserted .... and .... He denied ....'. and implied that ....

Synonyms

Look at these sentences:

> The Council has decided not to use the site in George Street. A new site has been found in East Street.
>
> The Council has decided not to use the site in George Street. A new location has been found in East Street.

You can avoid monotonous repetition by using a synonym. Find other synonyms in the speeches at the start of this unit.

Rewrite the second sentence of each of these pairs of sentences, using synonyms to avoid repetition:

1 There are many people who need work in the town. This project will provide work for them.
2 The council are going to build a new town hall. It will be built on the site in George Street.
3 The project will not be a waste of money. On the contrary, it will be a valuable investment of public money.
4 The project will be of lasting benefit. It will be of benefit not only to those directly concerned, but to the general public as well.
5 I am totally opposed to Councillor Harper's suggestion. The suggestion that we should build a new hall on this site would entail abandoning the plans for the park.

PARAGRAPH OUTLINE

The argument in both speeches in the reading passage is organised like this:

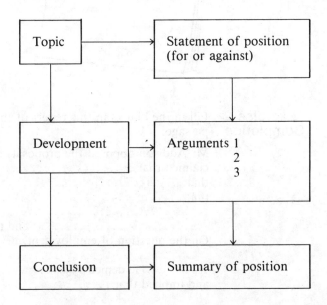

84

Exercise 3
Reordering

(i) Here are some notes for a speech opposing the plans to construct a third London airport at Stanstead:

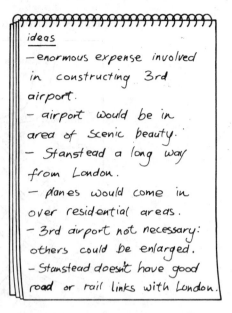

ideas
—enormous expense involved in constructing 3rd airport.
— airport would be in area of scenic beauty.
— Stanstead a long way from London.
— planes would come in over residential areas.
— 3rd airport not necessary: others could be enlarged.
— Stanstead doesn't have good road or rail links with London.

Reorganise the notes under the following headings:

Distance and inconvenience
Expense
Environmental issues

These headings correspond to the arguments in the 'Development' sentences of the paragraph outline.

Guided writing

(ii) Now use the notes to write out the speech in full.
Add an introductory statement summarising your position, and a conclusion offering alternative suggestions.

Exercise 4
Free writing

Local elections
Do this activity in pairs.
You are standing for election for the local council of your home town (or the town where you are studying if you are away from home).
Think about the town. What policies would you like to see adopted? What improvements would you like to see? Plan a speech putting forward your ideas and write notes for it.
When you have finished, leave your partner and get into a group of four other people.
Act out an election meeting in which each of you in turn puts forward his/her ideas.
Take notes while the others are speaking and write up a report afterwards.

Exercise 5
Role play

Do this activity in groups of six. Read the background information first.

This is Millford town centre.

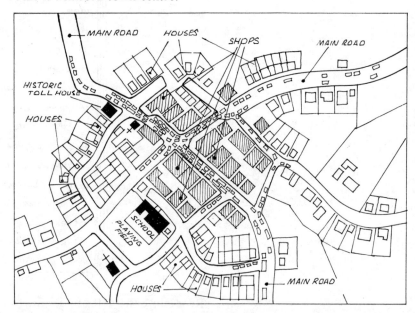

The town centre is at the junction of two main roads. It is very busy and there are often bad traffic jams, particularly at weekends and in the summer, when a lot of traffic passes through the town. The Town Council want to introduce a one-way system in the town to speed up the flow of traffic. Here is their proposed map:

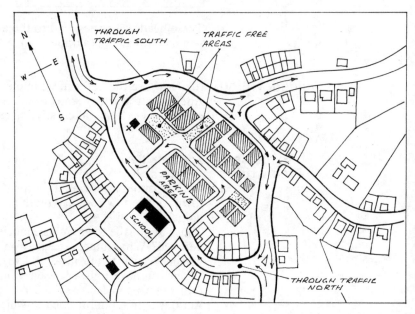

The one-way system would lead to a free flow of traffic in the town and prevent hold-ups.

Unfortunately there are a number of objections to this proposal. These come from:

(i) shopkeepers in Millford town centre who feel they will lose trade if traffic is diverted from the town centre

(ii) residents of the houses which would be pulled down to make the road wider

(iii) parents of children who would have to cross the new road to go to school

(iv) conservationists who are worried about the possibility of historic buildings being pulled down to make room for the wider roads.

The Council have therefore arranged a meeting so that those with objections can air their grievances.

Student A should look at Activity D on page 127.

B	"	"	"	"	E	"	"	127
C	"	"	"	"	L	"	"	130
D	"	"	"	"	P	"	"	131
E	"	"	"	"	S	"	"	133
F	"	"	"	"	V	"	"	134

Prepare notes for a speech outlining your point of view.

When everyone is ready, act out the meeting.

While the others are speaking, take notes on what they are saying and then use these notes to write up a full account of the meeting for the *Millford Daily Herald*.

Unit 14 How it's made

Describing processes

Using the passive

Reading Read the explanation of how paper is made. Complete the flow chart showing the stages in the process.

Paper

Modern paper is manufactured from a mixture of various fibres, including wood, grass and cotton.

When the logs arrive at the factory, the bark is removed. The wood is then fed into a mill in order to grind it to a pulp. A great deal of water and various vegetable fibres are added at this stage. The pulp is bleached and then beaten to break it down still further. Glue and resin are mixed with the pulp so that a better consistency is obtained. Next it is poured on to wire screens and rolled with the purpose of removing the water. It is then pressed and watermarked. It is subsequently dried and glazed so as to obtain a smooth finish.

Finally, it is reeled on to long rollers and cut to size.

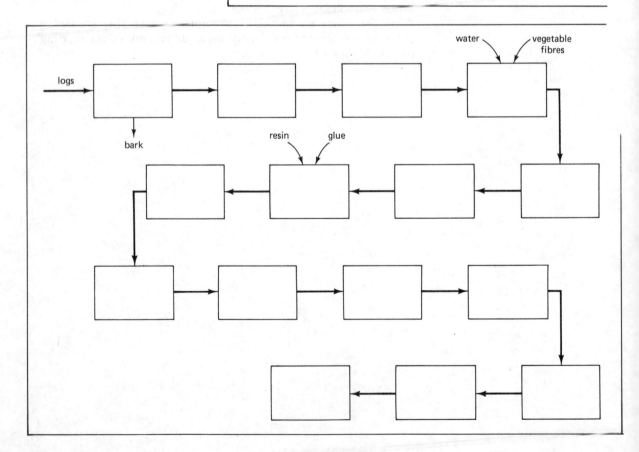

LANGUAGE SUMMARY 1   When you are writing an *explanation of a process* you will need to use a lot of *passive verbs*. The passive verbs make the text more *formal* and *impersonal* by removing all personal subjects. People are not important in processes, only actions.

2   Linking words for time relations (processes)
When you are explaining processes, you will need to show when *one action happens after another* and when *two actions happen at the same time*. The following table summarises some linking words for *processes*.

(i) One action after another

The pulp is bleached	{ **and** **and then** **and subsequently**	beaten.
	. In the next stage	it is beaten.
After { bleaching being bleached		it is beaten. the pulp is beaten.
When the pulp has been bleached		it is beaten.

(ii) Two simultaneous actions

The wood is fed into a mill.	Water is added	**at this stage.**
	At the same time	water is added.

3   Linking words for purpose
Finally, you will need to explain the *purpose* of some, or all of the stages in the process. The following table summarises some *linking words for expressing purpose*.

The pulp is beaten	**to** **so as to** **in order to**	break it down.
	so that	it is broken down.
	with the purpose of	breaking it down.

Exercise 1
Rewriting

The passage below is an informal talk on glass-making. It uses *we* and active verbs. Rewrite the passage for an official leaflet on glass-making. Make it more formal. Avoid using *we*.

> 'Well, first of all, we mix sand, soda, limestone, dolomite and feldspar in the mixer. Then we transfer them to the tank furnace. There we heat them to a temperature of about 1500°C and when the glass is liquid, we reduce the temperature to about 900°C and add arsenic and manganese dioxide. This removes discolouration. Then we pass the liquid glass through rollers and form it into sheets. When the glass is in the required shape, we cool it slowly. This stops it cracking.'

Exercise 2
Combining

(i) The half-sentences in column I describe *stages in the paper-making process*. The half sentences in Column II explain the *purpose of these stages*. Match each stage in Column I with its purpose in Column II. Refer to the reading passage to help you. Then join the two halves of each sentence with a linking word from the table in the language summary 3 (*Linking words for purpose*).

I	II
The wood is fed into a mill	break it down still further
The pulp is beaten	a better consistency is obtained
Glue and resin are mixed into the pulp	grind it into a pulp
The paper is dried and glazed	removing the bark
The pulp is rolled	obtain a smooth finish

Joining

(ii) Here are some notes that a student took during the talk on glass-making. Write them out in full. Use *Linking words for purpose* to join the two halves of the sentences.

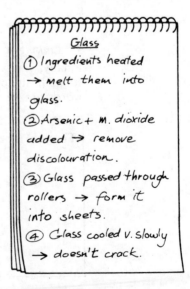

Glass
1. Ingredients heated
→ melt them into glass.
2. Arsenic + M. dioxide added → remove discolouration.
3. Glass passed through rollers → form it into sheets.
4. Glass cooled v. slowly → doesn't crack.

Reference exercise   **This/these**

You can use **this** or **these** to refer back and avoid repetition.
Look at these sentences:

> Petrol is passed through charcoal and earth. Charcoal and earth remove impurities.
>
> Petrol is passed through | charcoal and earth | . | These | remove impurities.

> The glass is cooled slowly. Cooling it slowly prevents it cracking.
>
> The glass is | cooled slowly | . | This | prevents it cracking.

Use **this** or **these** to refer back and to avoid repetition in the following pairs of sentences:
1   The porcelain cups are glazed. Glazing makes them watertight.
2   The pulp is beaten. Beating breaks it down.
3   Glue and resin are mixed with the wood pulp. Glue and resin give it a better consistency.
4   Chemicals are added to the petrol. The chemicals reduce odour.
5   The wood pulp is rolled. Rolling removes the water.

PARAGRAPH OUTLINE   A process description may begin with a sentence or two summarising the process (*Petrol is manufactured from crude oil by a process called refining.*) or by listing the materials used to make the finished product. (*Modern paper is manufactured from a mixture of various fibres including wood, grass and cotton.*) The various stages in the process are then described in order.
Linking words will be important here to show whether the stages occur one after the other or at the same time.

Exercise 3   (i) The following passage is in muddled order. Rewrite it with the
Reordering   stages in the correct order:

> **Petrol**
> It is then heated to a temperature of 300°C in order to distil off various gases.
> After heating, the oil is passed through charcoal or earth so as to absorb any impurities.
> The crude oil is fed into a sedimentation tank where the impurities are allowed to settle.
> It is allowed to cool.
> Finally, chemicals are added to reduce odour and to make the petrol resistant to ageing.
> It is subsequently reheated to a higher temperature to distil off various grades of oil.
> Petrol is manufactured from crude oil by a process called refining.

Guided writing   (ii) Look at the flow chart below showing how porcelain is made. Write an explanation of the process using the following framework:

First .... Then .... and .... at this stage. After this .... and .... Subsequently .... and .... After the first firing .... and .... Finally ....

Porcelain

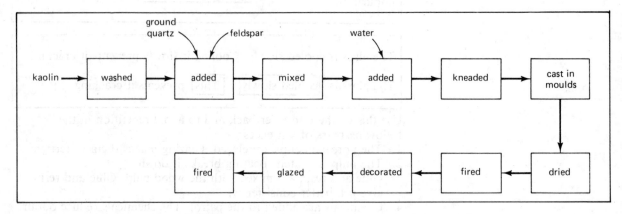

Exercise 4   Look at the flow chart below showing how rubber is made.
Free writing   Write an explanation of the rubber-making process.

Rubber

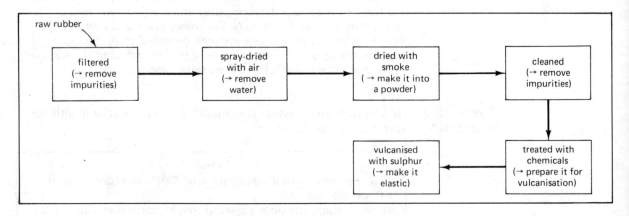

Exercise 5   Do this activity in pairs.
Writing activity

Student A's task	**Student B's task**
Look at Activity T on page 133. Describe to B how tea is produced and ask him to fill in his *blank* flow chart as you talk to him.	Look at Activity M on page 130. Describe to A how coffee is produced and ask him to fill in his *blank* flow chart as you talk to him.

When you have finished, use the notes you made during the talk to write an explanation of the process.

Unit 15 Changes

Expressing increase and decrease

Organising a factual report chronologically and under headings

Reading Read the following passage and use the information to help you plot the graph:

Britain's falling birth-rate

The birth-rate has dropped sharply recently to its lowest-ever figure of 600,000 births a year.

The average birth-rate before the First World War was around one million births a year. During the war years, 1914–1918, the birth-rate decreased dramatically but, at 800,000 births a year, was still higher than the present rate. With the post-war baby boom in the early 1920s, the birth-rate shot up to its highest-ever rate of 1,200,000 births a year, but by 1925 had declined to about 700,000 births a year. It remained at this rate during the war years 1939–1945, but rose steeply again in the post-war years to around one million births a year in 1948. There was a sharp drop in the mid 50s to 800,000 births, followed by a marked rise to a peak of one million in 1965. Since then the birth-rate has been declining steadily, until today, at its present level, it is lower than the death-rate for the first time in peacetime.

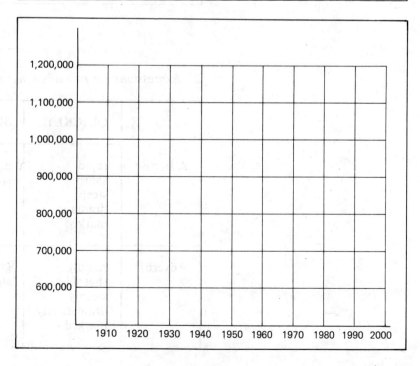

LANGUAGE SUMMARY When you are reporting changes, you will need to say

(i)   *how* something has changed (ie whether it has *increased* or *decreased*)
(ii) *how quickly or slowly* it changed and
(iii) *when* the change occurred.

The following tables summarise expressions for *increase and decrease, rate of change* and *duration of time*.

1 Expressions for increase and decrease

	UP	DOWN
Noun	a rise an increase an upward trend	a fall a decrease a reduction a decline a drop
Verb	to increase to shoot up } *implies quickly* to soar up	to decrease to drop to decline to fall to plunge *implies quickly*

2 Expressions for rate of change

	QUICKLY	SLOWLY
Adjective	rapid sharp steep dramatic marked	gradual steady
Adverb	rapidly sharply steeply dramatically markedly	gradually steadily

3 Linking words for time relations: duration of time

(i) Up to the present

Since			
	April 1976	onwards	there has been no change in the rate of inflation.
From			
For Over the last	two years six months		
Up till now So far			

(ii) Finished period

For	two years	
Up to	April September	there was no change in the rate of inflation.
During		
From	April to July	

Exercise 1
Matching

(i) Match the descriptions to the graphs:
1 There has recently been a marked decrease in the number of cigarette smokers.
2 Over the last few years there has been a steady reduction in the number of cinema-goers.
3 Sales shot up last month for the first time since April.
4 Inflation has risen steeply again this month.
5 There has been a general upward trend in the number of people purchasing TV licences.

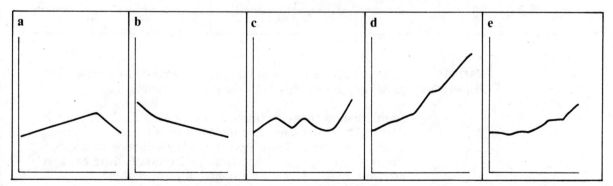

(ii) Match these descriptions with the graphs:
1 Since April last year there has been a marked rise in productivity.
2 For the last three months there has been an upward trend in car sales.
3 Up till now there has been a steady rise in prices.
4 The trade figures up to June last year showed a slight upward trend.
5 From 1976 onwards, inflation has risen dramatically.
6 Over the last three years there has been a gradual drop in the number of road accidents. At the same time, the number of vehicle owners has continued to rise.

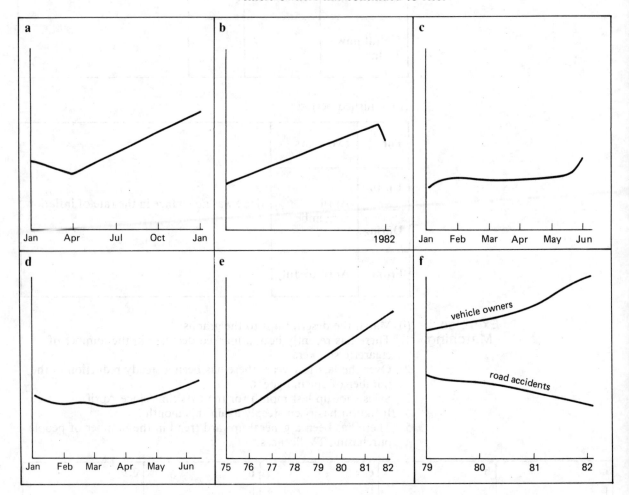

Exercise 2
Completion

(i) Use the information in the graph **a** opposite to complete the passage. Use language from the language summary.

Statistics show that consumption of coal has .... since 1952. At the same time there has been a .... in oil consumption. From 1962 onwards production of nuclear electricity has .... and from 1972 onwards there has also been an .... in the consumption of natural gas.

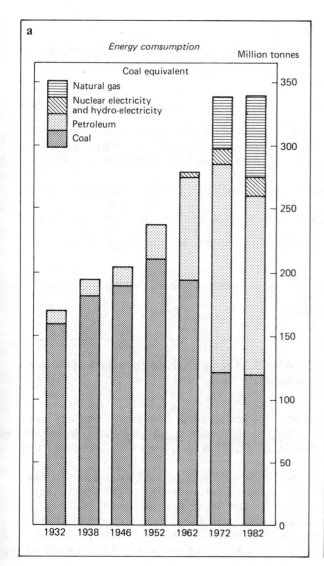

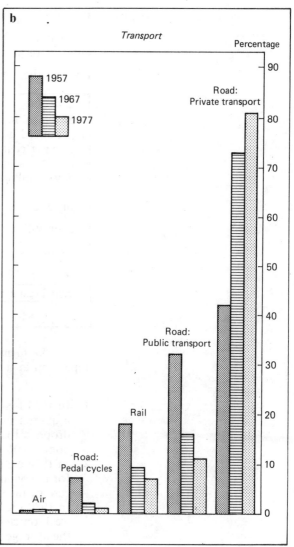

(ii) Use the information in the graph **b** above to help you choose the best phrase to fill in the blanks.

since 1957
over the last thirty years
at the same time
from 1957 onwards

.... there has been a gradual increase in the number of air passengers .... the number of those using public transport fell, but .... there has been a marked increase in the number of private vehicle owners.

Reference exercise

Former/latter/respectively

You can refer back and avoid repetition by using **the former, the latter** or **respectively**.

Look at these sentences:

> Seven million tons of iron and thirty million tons of steel were produced in 1973. In 1979 production of iron fell by twenty-five per cent and production of steel fell by twenty per cent.
>
> Seven million tons of iron and thirty million tons of steel were produced in 1973. In 1979 production of the ⌐former⌐ fell by twenty-five per cent and production of ⌐the latter⌐ fell by twenty per cent.
>
> In 1979 production fell by twenty-five per cent and twenty per cent ⌐respectively⌐ .

Use **the former, the latter** or **respectively** to refer back and avoid repetition in these sentences:

1 In 1974 two million cars were produced for export and one and a quarter million for the home market. In 1975 these figures dropped to a quarter of a million for export and 750,000 for the home market.
2 In 1974 average weekly earnings were £73.89 for a man and £44 for a woman. In 1978 these figures rose by ten per cent in the case of men and five per cent in the case of women.
3 In 1980 the average family spent £28 a week on food and £15 a week on clothes. In 1982 expenditure rose by eleven per cent; the average family spent £30 a week on food and £17 a week on clothes.
4 In 1962 Britain consumed 200 million tons of coal and 175 million tons of petroleum. By 1972 consumption of coal had fallen by 80 million tons while consumption of petroleum had increased by 100 million tons.
5 In 1968 Britain consumed 127 million gallons of spirits and 46 million gallons of wine. In 1978 Britain consumed 36 million gallons of spirits and 92 million gallons of wine.

Exercise 3
Guided writing

Study the graph opposite and write a passage describing the changes in crop production in Britain.
You can arrange the information either in chronological order (paragraph outline A), or following the crops from left to right on the chart (paragraph outline B).

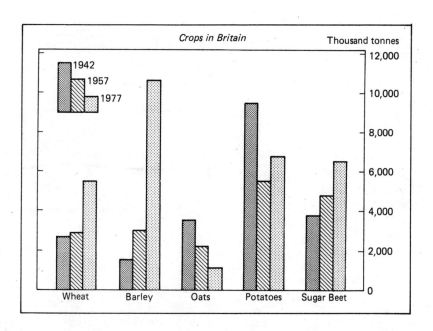

Crops in Britain

PARAGRAPH OUTLINE

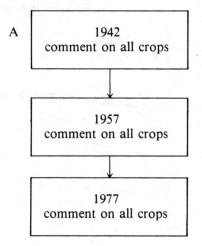

A
1942
comment on all crops

1957
comment on all crops

1977
comment on all crops

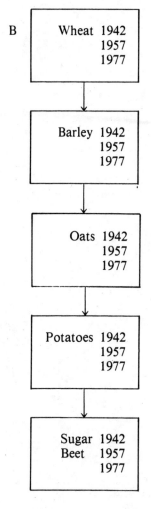

B
Wheat 1942
1957
1977

Barley 1942
1957
1977

Oats 1942
1957
1977

Potatoes 1942
1957
1977

Sugar 1942
Beet 1957
1977

Exercise 4
Free writing

Study the following graph.
Write a short account of the trends and changes that have occurred.

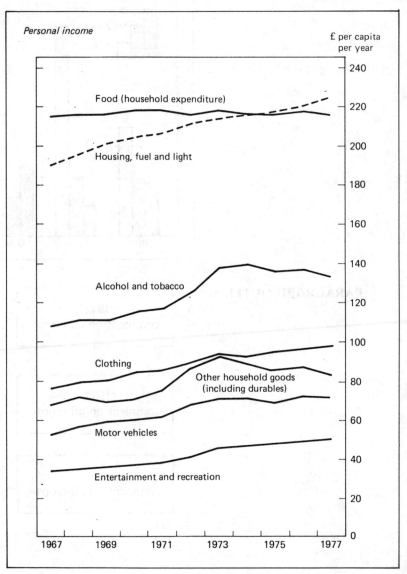

Exercise 5
Writing activity

Make a survey to find how fashions have changed in the last ten years. Ask other members of your class what they wore ten years ago, what they wore five years ago, and what they wear now. Find out whether there has been a rise or fall in the number of people wearing:

| miniskirts | beards | long hair | high heels |
| long dresses | earrings | jeans | ties suits |

Make a chart and then write an account of your findings.

Unit 16 Letters to the Editor

Organising argument: points for and against

Reading   Read the following letters from the *Eastcliffe Gazette*.

Sir,

   I cannot agree with the Council's proposals to cut back library services in the area. There are no good bookshops in Eastcliffe, and besides, many people rely on libraries to supply books that they could never afford to buy. Although the Mobile Library Service may be expensive to run, many elderly people in country areas are unable to go to the Central Library, and to abandon the service would be to deprive them of one of life's few remaining pleasures. In my view this is an unwise decision, which should be reconsidered.

Sir,

   I thoroughly approve of the Government's proposal to reintroduce military service. In my view, youngsters these days simply do not know how fortunate they are: the State provides everything they need, and they give nothing back in return. Furthermore, two years in the army would teach them a sense of responsibility to society, a quality which is sadly lacking today — many youths instead turn to violence, witness the recent riots in our inner cities.

Sir,

   I wish to register a protest about your article on Tuesday ('Bonzo the Boozer'). While it is true that my dog is big and black, it is untrue to suggest that he is fierce and aggressive. He has never, to my knowledge, attacked any customers. On the contrary, he likes his pint, and many of my regular customers buy him drinks. I invite any of your readers to come along and see for themselves!

Sir,

   I would like to protest about the Council's recent decision to cut bus services in rural areas. Though it is true that many people nowadays have cars, those who can't afford to run one will suffer. Moreover, in view of the world petrol crisis, we need to start pooling our resources, and use our energy for the benefit of all.

Who do you think wrote these letters? Match each of the signatures below with the appropriate letter.

Col. Smythe

Col. Smythe, ex army officer

Peace Hooper.

Lady Peace Hooper, Secretary of the Literary Guild

Fred Jarvis

Fred Jarvis, landlord of the Pig and Whistle Inn

Martha Berry

Martha Berry, Treasurer of Eastcliffe Ecology Group

LANGUAGE SUMMARY   The language used in letters to a newspaper is usually formal and
dignified in tone. Most letters begin by stating the writer's position,
expressing his *approval* or *disapproval* of a particular subject.

The following table summarises some ways of introducing a letter
to a newspaper.

1   Introductory statements

Expressing approval	I welcome I thoroughly approve of I am writing to express my approval of I would like to express my support for
Expressing disapproval	I cannot agree with I do not believe that I strongly disagree with I would like to protest about

The main part of a letter to a newspaper will contain arguments for
and against the subject. The writer will express his own opinion
(*make points in support of his argument*) and discuss other people's
opinions (*dealing with points contrary to his argument*). He may
either admit that these opinions are right, but argue that his own
are more important (*conceding*), or he may state that other
opinions are wrong, and his own opinions are right (*refuting*).
Linking words are very important in argument because they show
the relationship between a writer's ideas. The following table
summarises some linking words for an argument.

2   Linking words for argument
(i) Making points in support of your argument

Not only is	the project very costly	it is **also**	totally unnecessary.
	The project is very costly.	**Moreover** **Besides** **What is more** **In addition** **Furthermore**	it is totally unnecessary.

(ii) Dealing with points contrary to your argument

Conceding			
Although **In spite of the** **fact that**	the building is very costly		it has been necessary for some time.
	The building is very costly.	**However** **Nevertheless** **Still** **Yet**	

Refuting		
The building will not be costly.	**On the contrary,**	the cost will be very low.

(iii) Concluding an argument
The last sentence of a letter to a newspaper usually summarises
the writer's position, or makes a suggestion. Here are some *linking
words* for *conclusions*:

| Finally |
| In conclusion |
| To sum up |
| Therefore |

Exercise 1
Matching

Unfortunately, the Editor of the *Torbury Exress* tore up the letters
that were supposed to be printed in Friday's paper. His secretary
found these fragments in the wastepaper basket. Can you match the
sentences and join them with an appropriate linking word?

I strongly disagree with most of Mr Smythe's proposals

The new buildings are extremely ugly

The policies of the new Government have led to a massive increase in unemployment

The large new schools can offer a wide variety of subjects

Prisons do not reform young offenders

they are a total waste of money

they have caused a rise in inflation

they often make them into hardened criminals

their size can lead to feelings of anonymity

there is one point on which I am in total agreement

Exercise 2
Completion

Read the following letters which express opposing viewpoints on the Government's proposals to introduce retirement at fifty-five years old.

(i) Fill in the blanks in these two letters, using linking words from the language summary to join the ideas together and make the letters flow more smoothly.

(ii) Add introductory and concluding statements to complete both letters.

Sir,

. . . .
. . . .
It is true that the introduction of early retirement would provide more opportunities for younger people. . . . . this would lead to a young and inexperienced workforce. I do not believe that people in general would welcome early retirement . . . . most people enjoy working and do not know how to use their leisure . . . . the tax necessary to provide all the extra pensions would have to come from workers' salaries
. . . .
. . . .

Sir,

. . . .
. . . .
More young people will be able to get jobs and, ... , promotion will not be so restricted. People in their fifties are ready to retire and will get more out of their retirement than those who retire later. . . . . there is a danger that people will become bored and provision must therefore be made for better leisure facilities . . . .
. . . .

Reference exercise

This/these/such a/such

You can use **this** or **these** and a synonym to refer back and to avoid repetition. You can also use **such a** or **such** which make your style formal and dignified in tone.
Look at these sentences:

I am writing to protest about the new suggestions for introducing military service.
These | proposals seem impractical and ill-considered.
Such |

I am writing to protest about the new proposal to introduce military service. Such a | plan seems impractical and
                            This | ill-considered.

Use **this/these** and a synonym to refer back and avoid repetition in these sentences:

1 I am writing to register a protest about the Council's plans to cut bus services. The plans seem very short-sighted.
2 I thoroughly approve of the new system of local government. The system is a great improvement on the old one.
3 The Council have approved plans to build a new arts centre in the town. The new arts centre would contain an art gallery and a cinema as well as a theatre.
4 I am writing to protest about the proposed changes to be made to the library services. The changes are neither necessary nor desirable.
5 I am writing to protest about the proposed rise in local taxes. The rise will cause hardship to many people.

PARAGRAPH OUTLINE   A letter expressing your point of view will begin with a sentence or two summarising your opinion. It will list the arguments supporting your point of view and reject those against it. It may end by restating your viewpoint, or by offering suggestions for action.

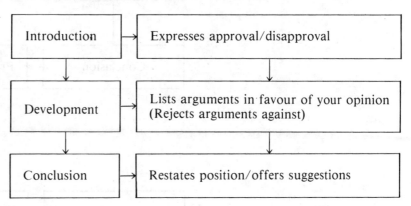

Introduction	→	Expresses approval/disapproval
Development	→	Lists arguments in favour of your opinion (Rejects arguments against)
Conclusion	→	Restates position/offers suggestions

Exercise 3   (i) The following letter is in muddled order. Use the paragraph
Reordering   outline to help you rewrite it in a more coherent order.

Sir,

Crime and vandalism would be reduced as a result.

The proposals should therefore be introduced without delay.

Moreover, it would encourage a community spirit and a sense of responsibility towards other members of society.

I am writing to express my approval of the Government's proposal to introduce a year's compulsory Community Service for school leavers.

This would act as a bridge between school and work, helping to prepare school leavers for employment.

                    Yours faithfully,

                    J. P. Hunter

Guided writing (ii) Now follow the suggested outlines and write a) Mr Simmond's reply to Mr Hunter's letter, b) Mr Hunter's reply to Mr Simmond's letter.

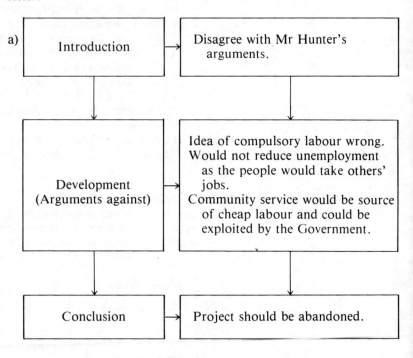

a)

| Introduction → | Disagree with Mr Hunter's arguments. |

| Development (Arguments against) → | Idea of compulsory labour wrong. Would not reduce unemployment as the people would take others' jobs. Community service would be source of cheap labour and could be exploited by the Government. |

| Conclusion → | Project should be abandoned. |

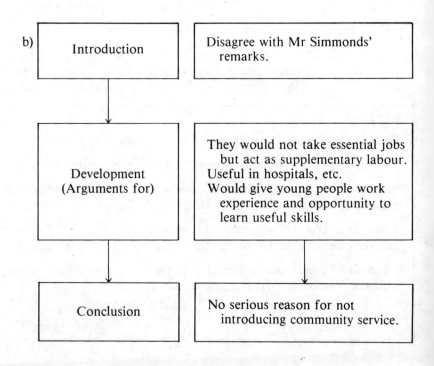

b)

| Introduction | Disagree with Mr Simmonds' remarks. |

| Development (Arguments for) | They would not take essential jobs but act as supplementary labour. Useful in hospitals, etc. Would give young people work experience and opportunity to learn useful skills. |

| Conclusion | No serious reason for not introducing community service. |

Exercise 4
Free writing   Reread the letters in the reading section. Write a reply to each letter expressing the *opposite* viewpoint.

Exercise 5
Writing activity   (i) Do this activity in groups of eight. Read the *background information* first.

> Amesford Town Council is seriously short of money.
> They propose to save money next year by:
> cutting the education budget by 10%
> abandoning plans to build a new youth centre.
> Money could however be saved in *other ways:*
> local taxes (rates) could be increased
> the plans to build a new arts centre containing theatre, concert
>   hall, art gallery, could be dropped.

Now divide your group into eight pairs.

> Students A and B should look at Activity B on page 126
>   C and D   "   "   H "   "   128
>   E and F   "   "   K "   "   129
>   G and H   "   "   N "   "   131

Each pair should prepare their roles together for ten minutes.
Then call a public meeting in which all eight of you will express your views. Appoint a chairman.
When you have finished, write a letter to your local newspaper, expressing your point of view.

(ii) Is there anything happening in your town which makes you pleased, or angry? Write a letter about it to the newspaper.

Unit 17 Opinion poll

Organising a report: generalisations and facts

Expressing proportion

Reading   Read the following text and use the information in it to complete the tables below.

> The results of a new survey indicate that most people are not motivated to work hard.
>
> The survey suggests that most full-time workers do not wish to work harder than they do at present, and are interested in more leisure rather than extra money. This is shown by the fact that 51% of those questioned said they would not work longer hours even for more money.
>
> The majority of workers, 56%, said that they could not work more efficiently than at present, but over four out of ten admitted that it would be possible for them to do so. Over half the employees said they had no ambition to be rich, and 45% did not regard themselves as having any ambition at all. This suggests that a substantial number of workers could work harder than they do, but have little drive or ambition and would not work harder even if they were paid much more.
>
> However, there is serious evidence for the view that this lack of motivation is not due to boredom or low wages. Only 5% of workers, for instance, found their jobs boring or hated their work, while only 10% gave low wages as a reason for lack of effort. A significantly larger proportion of workers, in contrast, blamed old fashioned equipment, while three out of ten workers identified inefficiency with poor management or bad organisation. By far the largest proportion of workers, however, put the blame on heavy taxation. These findings imply that the main reasons for the lack of will to work are to be found in external factors rather than in dissatisfaction with the job itself.
>
> These findings suggest that more effort should be put into improving conditions in factories and making their organisation more efficient. In addition, reducing taxation might do more than an increase in wages to increase workers' motivation.

Table 1

	YES	NO
Would you work longer hours for less money?		

Table 2

	YES	NO
Could you work more efficiently?		
Do you have an ambition to be rich?	35%	
Do you see yourself as having any ambition?		

Table 3   What is the main reason for your lack of motivation?

Work boring/hate my job		
Wages too low		
Equipment old fashioned	15%	
Poor management/bad organisation		
Taxation too heavy		

LANGUAGE SUMMARY
When you report the results of a survey, you will have to (i) report the figures you gathered (usually in the form of percentages and proportions) and (ii) make generalisations about those figures.
The following tables summarise ways of reporting figures (expressing *proportion*) and making *generalisations*.

1 Expressing proportions
Proportions may be expressed precisely in the form of percentages (45%, 25%, etc) or by using an expression such as 'one in two', or 'five out of ten'. Vague expressions such as 'a large number' can also be used. In general, unless absolute accuracy is very important it is better not to confuse your reader with too many percentages and figures.

VAGUE	most ↓ least	by far the largest proportion the majority a significantly larger proportion a large proportion a large number a substantial number a significant number a minority	of	people
PRECISE		51%		
		half the one in two five out of ten		

2 Linking words for facts and generalisations

The facts you have obtained in the survey can lead you to make a general remark. You can either (i) state the facts first and then make a generalisation about them *or* (ii) make your generalisation first and then produce the facts to support it. The following table shows ways of linking generalisation and fact.

(i) Facts before generalisation

'51% of people said they would not work longer hours for more money.'		
This indicates/suggests/implies The implications of this are	that	most people would rather have more leisure than more money.

(ii) Generalisation before facts

'Most people would rather have more leisure than more money.'			
This is	indicated shown demonstrated illustrated exemplified	by	the fact that 51% of people said ...
An illustration of this is The evidence for this is comes from			the results of a survey in which 51% of people said ...
51%, for instance, said that ...			

Exercise 1
Rewriting

Most of the data you obtain will be in figures (eg *6 people out of 74* ...). You will have to express this more neatly, in the form of proportions. Find one *vague* expression and one *precise* expression in each case to report these figures.

1 25 people out of 75 said 'yes' to the question.
2 40 people thought the proposals were a good idea while 10 thought they were a bad idea.
3 15 people agreed with the suggestion while 25 disagreed.
4 35 people out of 130 said 'no' to the question.
5 24 people agreed while 40 disagreed.

Exercise 2
Combining

Choose expressions from the language summary to link facts and generalisations in these sentences.

1 In a survey conducted yesterday, 60% of people questioned said they would vote for the Opposition in the next election. The majority of voters are unhappy with the present government.
2 People are generally more affluent now than they were ten years ago. In 1972 only 65% of people owned a washing machine, compared with 81% today.
3 People are, in general, more mobile now than they were twenty years ago. 60% of people said they had moved away from their home town to work. The same response was given by only 40% of the population twenty years ago.
4 One in five youngsters between the ages of 13 and 17 has been convicted of an offence such as shoplifting, and one in thirty has been convicted of a more violent offence. There is a growth in crime amongst school children.
5 Most people enjoy their jobs. 75% of people said they were happy in their work.

Reference exercise

That/those
You can use **that** or **those** to refer back and to avoid repetition.
Look at these sentences:

The answers given by men were very different from the answers given by women.

The answers given by men were very different from ⌐those⌐

given by women.

The opinion held by men on this subject was very different from the opinion held by women.
The opinion held by men on this subject was very different

from ⌐that⌐ held by women.

Use **that** or **those** to refer back and avoid repetition in the following sentences:
1 The result of the 1982 survey was very similar to the result of the 1981 survey.
2 The answers actually given were very different from the answers predicted.

3   This result seems to indicate that the views of the workers on
    the subject do not differ greatly from the views of the
    management.
4   Conditions today are very different from conditions fifty years
    ago.

PARAGRAPH OUTLINE   Look at the reading passage.
Underline the <u>FACTS.</u>

Now put a ring round the (GENERALISATIONS.)

Sometimes the order is

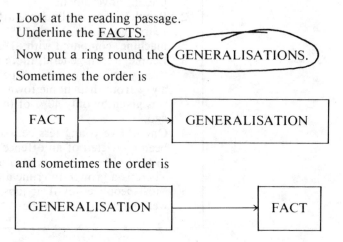

and sometimes the order is

Find an example of each in the passage.

A survey report may begin with a sentence summarising the most
important findings or conclusions of the survey, or by simply
stating the purpose of the survey. It may end with a general
conclusion, or with a recommendation or suggestion for action.

Exercise 3   (i) Below is a table showing how people spend their evenings and a
Rewriting   chart summarising generalisations and facts taken from the table.
1   Use the information in the table to fill in the blanks in the *facts*
    column. Use language from the language summary.
2   Draw a line to match generalisations and facts.
3   Decide on an order for the sentences, to make them into a
    coherent paragraph.

Reading	3%
Sport	5%
Cinema	10%
Theatre	3%

Concert	2%
Listening to records	3%
Evening classes	2%
Clubs or societies	2%
Political meetings	1%
Hobbies (at home)	5%
Entertaining or social	15%
Restaurant	5%
Watching TV	44%

Generalisations	Facts
The survey also revealed that more people prefer ready-made entertainment to entertainment they provide for themselves	Only . . . . of those questioned said they regularly practised a sport
A new survey revealed that the majority of people spend their evenings at home rather than in social or sporting activities outside the home	. . . . of those questioned said they spent their leisure time in such activities as watching TV, listening to records, reading or hobbies
Finally, it would seem that after a hard day's work people prefer not to engage in strenuous activity	. . . . people said they spent their time watching TV or going to the theatre, cinema or concerts, while only . . . . people said they had a regular hobby
For those who did go out in the evenings, social activities were more popular than cultural activities	. . . . people spent their evening entertaining or dining out while only . . . . people regularly went to the theatre, concerts or cinema

Guided writing   (ii) These are the answers to a survey on people's reasons for working:

What is you main reason for working?	
	%
To pay the bills	10
Get rich	5
Provide for children	40
Buy a house	5
Get promotion	5
Enjoy my job	35

These generalisations can be made on the basis of the facts:

> The main motivating factors for most people to work are personal satisfaction and family responsibilities.
>
> Ambition is not the main motivation for most people in their work.
>
> Surprisingly, money did not seem to play an important part in motivating people to work.

Add the supporting facts to each generalisation and join them together to form a paragraph. Add an introductory and a concluding sentence.

Exercise 4   The table opposite shows the results of a survey on people's ideal
Free writing   marriage partners. Write a report of the results of the survey, with one paragraph for the women's views and one for the men's.

My Ideal Partner has to be:

	Men	Women
	%	%
Romantic	20	65
Rich	30	40
Intelligent	20	30
Attractive	80	75
Kind	90	90
Successful	10	60
Sociable	60	30
Tolerant	90	90
Hardworking	25	75
Affectionate	95	95

Exercise 5
Writing activity

Choose one of the following subjects:

Food	Music
Work	Holidays
Television	The Future
Fears	Fashion
Travel	Money

Make up five questions to ask people in order to find out their opinions on the subject.
Then use your questions to take a class opinion poll on the subject.
Record your findings and use them to write a passage of generalisation about the people in your class.
Support your statements with facts.

Unit 18 Proposals

Making proposals and describing features

Organising a description in order of importance or under headings

Reading Here is a child's drawing of a more convenient and comfortable bicycle for postmen.

The passage below explains his proposals for improvements to the traditional bicycle. Read the passage and do the exercise which follows.

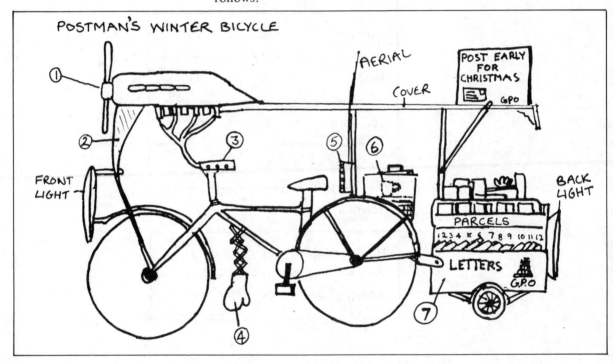

POSTMAN'S WINTER BICYCLE

The bicycle would have an engine and propellors to help it up steep hills, and a windscreen to keep rain and wind off the postman's face. There would be heated handlebars to keep the postman's hands warm in the cold weather. Another essential feature would be a boxing glove for getting rid of fierce dogs. There should be a radio to entertain the postman when he has to cycle long distances. This would be situated just behind the postman's seat. He could then play it quietly and not disturb other people. I think the bicycle should be equipped with a machine for making tea, so that the postman could have a cup of tea as often as he wanted. This should be placed on the back wheel so that he can reach it easily. There should be a trailer behind the bicycle to hold letters and parcels.

This is the key to the parts of the bicycle that are numbered.
Read the text and complete the key.
Number 1 has been done for you.

Number	Feature	Purpose
1	propellor	to help the bike up steep hills
2		to
3		to
4		for
5		to
6		for
7		to

LANGUAGE SUMMARY

When you are writing a proposal you will need to do two things:

(i) make suggestions for improvements or new features.

and

(ii) explain why you are suggesting these improvements, that is to explain the purpose of the improvements.

The following tables summarise ways of *making suggestions* and ways of *expressing purpose*.

1 Making suggestions
The words *should* and *would* in themselves express *suggestion*. You may like to introduce your suggestion with a phrase like *I propose that* ... This gives a very formal tone.

I would suggest
I propose
I would like to
   put forward
   the idea
	that	the bicycle	should have	a tea machine.

		there	should be	a tea machine.
		the machine		made of plastic.

The bicycle			have	a tea machine.
There An essential feature	should would		be	a tea machine.
The tea machine			be	equipped with cups. placed behind the seat. made of plastic.

117

2 Linking words for purpose

You can express the purpose of objects or features by using **for** + **ing** or **to** + **infinitive**, **so that** or **then**.

The bicycle would have a drinks machine	**for** making tea. **to** make tea. **so that** the postman could make tea. . The postman could **then** make tea.

Exercise 1
Matching

This is a another child's picture of a bicycle for postmen:

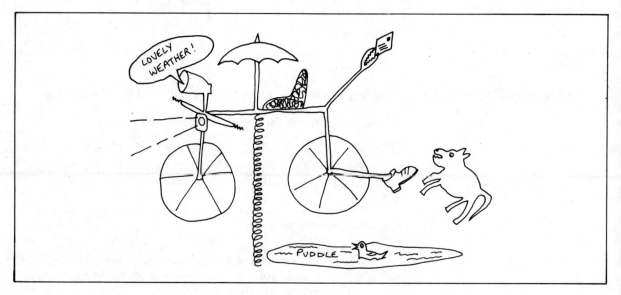

Match *feature* and *purpose* in the following table and connect them with:

to + **infinitive** or **for** + **ing**.

Then label the different parts of the bicycle.

Feature	Purpose
an automatic boot a spotlight an umbrella an automatic arm a spring attachment a centrally-heated sheepskin seat a conversation device	it jumps over puddles it keeps the rain off it kicks fierce dogs it lights up house numbers on dark evenings it posts letters it talks to householders it keeps the postman comfortable

Exercise 2
Completion

Use the language summary to help you fill in the blanks in this description of the second bicycle:

At the front, ... a conversation device for talking to householders, and a ....
....
    In the central areas, ... that the bicycle
.... equipped with a ....
.... and a ....
.... Another essential feature
.... an umbrella ....
....
    At the rear of the bicycle .... an automatic arm .... It would be a good idea
....
.... This .... on the rear wheel.

Reference exercise

One/another one/the other some/others
You can refer back and avoid repetition by using **one/another one/ the other or some/others (the others)**
Look at these sentences:

The robot would have two automatic arms . One would have a spade for gardening. The other would have a hook for carrying things.

The robot would have several automatic arms . One would be equipped with a spade for gardening. Another would have a hook for carrying things.

The robot would have several automatic arms . Some would be designed to perform household tasks. Others would be used for gardening.

> The robot would have four automatic arms. Two would be used for gardening. The others would perform simple household tasks.

Use **one, another, the other, some** or **(the) others** to refer back and avoid repetition in these sentences:

1 There would be several switches to the right of the driving wheel. Several switches would be situated on the dashboard.
2 There would be two theatres in the new arts complex. One theatre would put on plays for adults. One theatre would show plays for children.
3 The machine would have four sets of dials. One set would control the speed. Three sets would control direction and height.
4 The house would have ten rooms upstairs. A few rooms would be used as bedrooms. A few rooms could be used for work or hobbies.
5 The new bicycle would have several automatic devices. There would be a device for posting letters and a device for frightening dogs.

PARAGRAPH OUTLINE In the proposals for the bicycles, the bikes are described from end to end. You could also organise a list of features in other ways. You could, for example, list the features *in order of importance* or group them *under headings*, like this:

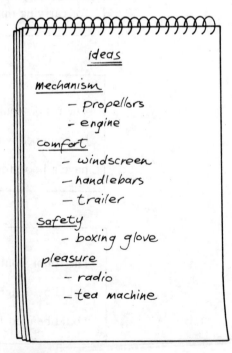

ideas

mechanism
    — propellors
    — engine
comfort
    — windscreen
    — handlebars
    — trailer
safety
    — boxing glove
pleasure
    — radio
    — tea machine

Exercise 3
Guided writing

(i) Reorganise the first passage into four short paragraphs, and write a letter to the Post Office setting out your proposals. Arrange it like this:

<table>
<tr><td></td><td>

5 Rose Street,
Cardiff.

15 December 1982

The Director-General,
The Post Office,
London.

Dear Sir,

</td></tr>
</table>

Introduction (purpose of letter) →	I am writing to suggest .....
Development (proposals) →	Certain mechanical improvements should be made to the bicycle ..... It is important that the postman should feel comfortable ..... Safety is also very important ..... Finally, the postman should have entertainment on his journey ......
Conclusion (ask for a reply) →	I hope you will give these proposals your full consideration. I look forward to hearing from you.

Yours faithfully,

S. R. Puttock

(ii) The pictures below are drawings of 'sleep machines', special beds for people who have trouble going to sleep. Follow the suggested outlines below, and write proposals for each bed. The features in picture a) are listed under *headings* and in picture b) in *order of importance*.

a)

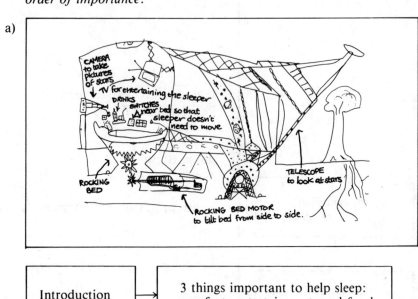

Introduction →	3 things important to help sleep: comfort, entertainment, and food.
Comfort Entertainment Food →	rocking motor/convenient switches telescope/camera/TV drinks near bed.

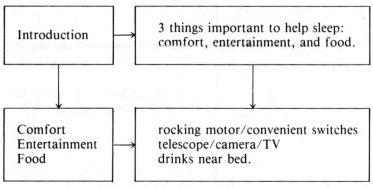

b)

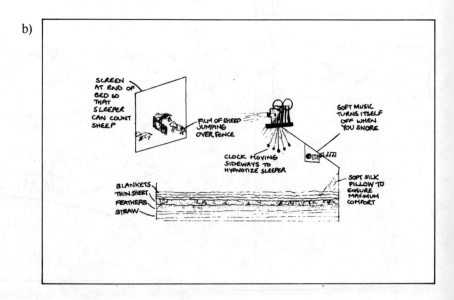

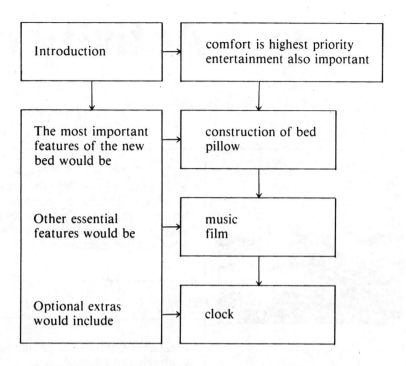

Exercise 4
Free writing

Imagine you are an architect.
You have to design a house for one of the following people:
(i) a sports fanatic
(ii) an animal lover
(iii) a magician

Draw a plan of the house, incorporating the special features you have designed.
Then write a formal letter to your client, outlining and explaining your proposals.

Exercise 5
Writing activity

(i) Do this activity in pairs.
Interview a partner about his likes and dislikes, hobbies and interests. Find out:
1   the three things he most dislikes
2   the three things he is most afraid of
3   the three daily activities he most dislikes doing.

Design a machine to make life easier for your partner. Show him the plan and explain your ideas.
If he approves, write a full proposal.
If he disapproves of anything, make alterations and then write your proposal.
(ii) Alternatively, work in groups of four.
Discuss each others' likes and dislikes, hobbies, and interests.
Design a house you would *all* like to live in.

Activity cards

A

POLICEMAN

Your job is to interview the drivers and witnesses. This picture shows the scene of the accident when you arrived. You should arrive on the scene five minutes after the start of the role play. Try to stay calm. Interview each person. Try to find out what *really* happened.

B

Mr James Chalford, (Headmaster of St Gudrun's, a local comprehensive school)
and Mr/Mrs Jo Clark (Governor of 2 local schools)

Points to consider:
1   there will be an increase in the school population over the next 5 years
2   St Gudrun's desperately needs a new library
3   the education budget was cut by 7.5% last year.

Discuss your opinions. What alternative suggestions could you make?

C

MOTHER/FATHER

You are very worried about your son/daughter, who is not working at all well at school, and who although sixteen years old is not the slightest bit interested in finding a job. A lot of badly-behaved friends are having a bad influence on him/her. You have spent a large part of your life bringing your child up, and cannot understand why you are now rejected. You only want two things — a bit more respect for the home, and some signs that he/she is thinking about a career. All he/she seems to be interested in is loud rock music. (Although you won't mention it directly, you are very worried about his/her girl/boy friend, and wish they'd stop seeing each other.)

Talk to your son/daughter, and then write a letter to a close friend asking for advice.

D

1   Mrs Peters (Representative of the Flower Hill Residents' Association)

Facts to consider:
1   20–30 houses would have to be pulled down to make room for the new roads
2   those on the other side of the large road would feel cut off from the town.

You want to know what proposals the Council has for rehousing. Look at the map. What alternative routes could you propose?

E

2   Mrs Mitchell (President of the Flower Hill Primary School Parent Teacher Association)

Facts to consider:
40% of the children going to Flower Hill Primary School would have to cross the new road if the one-way system were adopted.
You want to know what arrangements would be made for crossing patrols, etc. Look at the map. Can you suggest an alternative route?

F

DRIVER OF BLACK CAR   You were going up East Street behind the white car. These pictures show what happened:

Get out of your car. You are very angry. When the policeman arrives, make sure you tell him *your* story first.

G

FLATMATE 1

It's time you sorted things out, and brought everything into
the open! You have been sharing a flat for six months, and
though the first month was OK, things have been getting
worse — ever since the night you arrived back, tired out after
a long Friday at work, and found sixteen strangers piled on
top of each other in *your* room, drinking *your* coffee and
stubbing their cigarettes out in *your* coffee cups! Besides
which, they were playing loud rock music on *your* new stereo
system!

You are a quiet person who wishes no harm to anyone; all
you want is a quiet, tidy home to relax in after your busy day.
You like simple foods, and wear ordinary clothes, while your
flatmate is into exotic cuisine, wears the most outrageous
clothes, and always seems to have a new friend to invite back.
You don't want to move, but life is becoming unbearable. Sit
down and *talk* to your flatmate. Later, write a letter asking
for help from a close friend.

H

Tom and Tina Wright   }   Members of the local
Leslie and Lesley Phillips }   rate payers' association

Points to consider:
1   local taxes are now higher than ever before, and Amesford
    has the highest rates in the country
2   local feeling is strongly against raising rates
3   the Council will lose the elections next year if they raise
    rates any higher.

You would like to see all the new projects abandoned.

I

SON/DAUGHTER

You are sixteen years old, and you've had enough! Your
parents are so *boring*! School is a total waste of time, and
though you really would like to work when you leave school,
there just aren't any jobs; so it's better to enjoy life while you
can. You're very interested in music, and play lead guitar in a
rock band with some school friends. At least your friends are
interesting people — but then why can't your parents be a bit
more welcoming when you take them home? What you'd
really like are more interest from your parents in what you're
doing, and some proper advice from someone about what to
do when you leave school. You're very serious about your

girl/boy friend, but certainly wouldn't mention it to your parents unless forced to.

Talk to your father/mother, and then write a letter to a close friend asking for advice.

J

DRIVER OF THE WHITE CAR
You were going up East Street in front of the black car. These pictures show what happened:

Get out of your car and speak to the driver of the black car. You are very angry. When the policeman arrives, make sure he hears *your* story first.

K

Fred or Freda Wilson (Youth worker)
Viv Mumby (Social worker)

Points to consider:
1 there is nowhere for young people to go in the town
2 there is an increase in street crimes, violence and delinquency
3 old people are beginning to move out of Amesford because of the crime.

What is your opinion of the proposed budget?
What do *you* think should be done with the funds?

L

3 Mr Falconer (Representative for the local conservation association)

Facts to consider:
1 two fine old buildings would be pulled down to make room for the road
2 you feel the town would lose its charm if fast traffic were constantly passing through it.

Look at the map. What alternative suggestions could you make?

M

STUDENT B

Coffee production

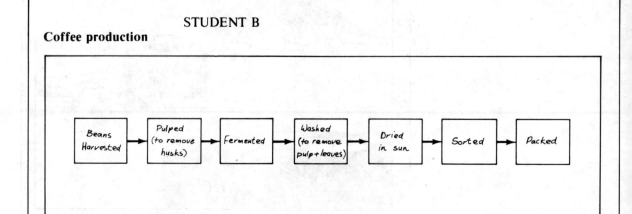

Tea production

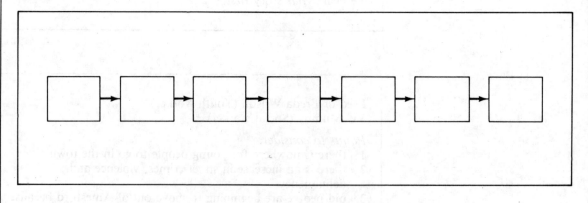

Phillip or Phyllis Cooper (Representative from the Arts Group)
Majorie Felixstowe or Mike Felixstowe (Secretary of the Literary Guild)

Points to consider:
1   there is no culture in this town; only one old cinema
2   a theatre/concert hall is desperately needed to replace the old Palace Hall which the Council pulled down 5 years ago
3   people would pay for better amenities.

What is your opinion of the proposed budget?
What suggestions can you make?

O

PASSENGER IN THE WHITE CAR
You were going up East Street in front of the *black* car. These pictures show what you think happened:

You feel very emotional and confused. You are not *exactly* sure what happened: it was all such a shock.

P

4   Mr Jones (Shopkeeper)

Points to consider:
1   many small shops would lose a lot of trade if traffic were diverted off the main street, or if it were passing through very fast.

2   you would like the system to remain as it is. You don't really see what is wrong with it. Find other arguments to support this view.

Q

FLATMATE 2

What's up with your flatmate? You've been perfectly happy for the past six months. All of a sudden, the atmosphere in the flat is strained and tense, and you now feel like a stranger in your own place. It may be because you have all the luck — you make friends easily, and you enjoy everything you do — and you can't understand at all how your flatmate can just sit there listening to boring classical music and drinking tea, instead of going out like you. *And* you found the flat in the first place, so what right has she/he to complain? However you are at heart a gentle, kind person, and you can see that deep down there may be a real problem ... Should you suggest going to see the doctor? However you wouldn't suggest this except as a last resort.

You certainly don't want to leave the flat — it's small, but comfortable. Perhaps your flatmate would be better off elsewhere?

Talk to him/her, then write a letter about it to a close friend asking for advice.

R

PEDESTRIAN

You were walking along to the corner of Hedge Lane when you saw the accident. These pictures show what happened:

Run and phone the police. Then come back and try to calm everybody down. Stay cool. You are an 'organiser'.

S

5 Mr Carter (Town planner)

Facts to consider:
1 in summer there are often queues for three miles
2 a bypass is an alternative, but it would be far more
   expensive.

You feel the situation can't go on like this and some people
will have to make sacrifices. Look at the map. Why do you
feel this is the best possible route for the one-way system?
Think of some reasons.

T

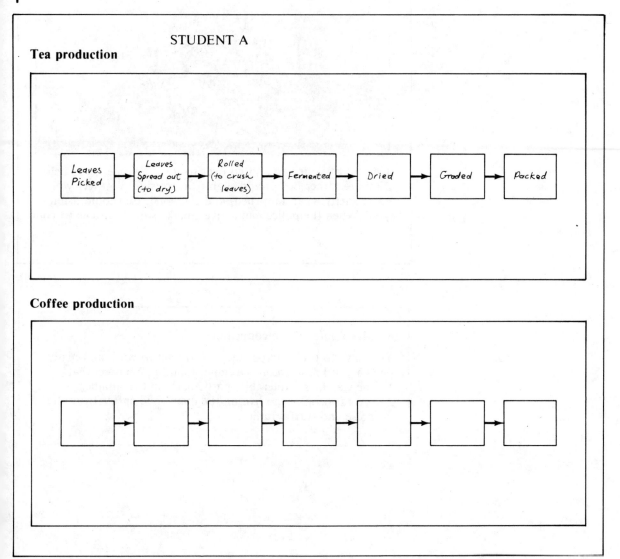

STUDENT A

Tea production

Leaves Picked → Leaves Spread out (to dry) → Rolled (to crush leaves) → Fermented → Dried → Graded → Packed

Coffee production

VAN DRIVER

You were driving your van along East Street when you saw an accident on the opposite side of the road. You only just managed to stop in time! These pictures show what happened:

Get out of your van and go over to see if anyone needs help. You are rather bossy, and slightly aggressive. You feel you saw exactly what happened, and everyone else should listen to you! When the policeman arrives, make sure he listens to your version.

V

6   Mrs White (Town councillor)

You have to travel across the town to get to work and many people you know are in the same situation. You feel that:
1   the traffic is intolerable, particularly in the summer
2   several people who live on the main road suffer from the noise and traffic fumes.